THE ANGLO-BOER WAR

Why Was It Fought?   Who Was Responsible?

PROBLEMS IN EUROPEAN CIVILIZATION

UNDER THE EDITORIAL DIRECTION OF

Ralph W. Greenlaw* and Dwight E. Lee†

DECLINE AND FALL OF THE ROMAN EMPIRE — *Why Did It Collapse?* †

THE PIRENNE THESIS — *Analysis, Criticism, and Revision**

THE CORONATION OF CHARLEMAGNE — *What Did It Signify?* *

THE GREGORIAN EPOCH — *Reformation, Revolution, Reaction?* *

INNOCENT III — *Vicar of Christ or Lord of the World?* †

THE CRUSADES — *Motives and Achievements**

THE RENAISSANCE — *Medieval or Modern?* *

MACHIAVELLI — *Cynic, Patriot, or Political Scientist?* *

THE REFORMATION — *Material or Spiritual?* *

THE "NEW MONARCHIES" AND REPRESENTATIVE ASSEMBLIES — *Medieval Constitutionalism or Modern Absolutism?* *

THE CHARACTER OF PHILIP II — *The Problem of Moral Judgments in History**

THE THIRTY YEARS' WAR — *Problems of Motive, Extent and Effect**

PROTESTANTISM AND CAPITALISM — *The Weber Thesis and Its Critics**

THE ORIGINS OF THE ENGLISH CIVIL WAR — *Conspiracy, Crusade, or Class Conflict?* *

THE REVOLUTION OF 1688 — *Whig Triumph or Palace Revolution?* †

PETER THE GREAT — *Reformer or Revolutionary?* †

THE GREATNESS OF LOUIS XIV — *Myth or Reality?* *

GEORGE III — *Tyrant or Constitutional Monarch?* *

THE EIGHTEENTH-CENTURY REVOLUTION — *French or Western?* †

THE INFLUENCE OF THE ENLIGHTENMENT ON THE FRENCH REVOLUTION — *Creative, Disastrous, or Non-Existent?* *

THE ECONOMIC ORIGINS OF THE FRENCH REVOLUTION — *Poverty or Prosperity?* *

METTERNICH, THE "COACHMAN OF EUROPE" — *Statesman or Evil Genius?* *

THE INDUSTRIAL REVOLUTION IN BRITAIN — *Triumph or Disaster?* *

ROMANTICISM — *Definition, Explanation and Evaluation* †

1848 — *A Turning Point?* *

NAPOLEON III — *Buffoon, Modern Dictator, or Sphinx?* †

OTTO VON BISMARCK — *A Historical Assessment**

IMPERIAL RUSSIA AFTER 1861 — *Peaceful Modernization or Revolution?* †

THE "NEW IMPERIALISM" — *Analysis of Late Nineteenth-Century Expansion**

THE ANGLO-BOER WAR — *Why Was It Fought? Who Was Responsible?* †

A FREE CHURCH IN A FREE STATE — *The Catholic Church, Italy, Germany, France, 1864–1914* †

THE DREYFUS AFFAIR — *A Tragedy of Errors?* †

THE OUTBREAK OF THE FIRST WORLD WAR — *Who Was Responsible?* *

THE RUSSIAN REVOLUTION AND BOLSHEVIK VICTORY — *Why and How?* *

THE VERSAILLES SETTLEMENT — *Was It Doomed to Failure?* *

THE STALIN REVOLUTION — *Fulfillment or Betrayal of Communism?* †

THE ETHIOPIAN CRISIS — *Touchstone of Appeasement?* *

THE NAZI REVOLUTION — *Germany's Guilt or Germany's Fate?* *

THE BRITISH IN INDIA — *Imperialism or Trusteeship?* †

THE OUTBREAK OF THE SECOND WORLD WAR — *Design or Blunder?* †

THE COLD WAR — *Ideological Conflict or Power Struggle?* †

Other volumes in preparation

PROBLEMS IN EUROPEAN CIVILIZATION

THE
ANGLO-BOER WAR

Why Was It Fought? Who Was Responsible?

Edited with an Introduction by

Theodore C. Caldwell,

UNIVERSITY OF MASSACHUSETTS

D. C. HEATH AND COMPANY · BOSTON

Englewood · Chicago · Dallas · San Francisco · Atlanta · London · Toronto

Table of Contents

I. A WAR TO PROTECT BRITISH SUBJECTS IN THE TRANSVAAL?

ARTHUR KEPPEL-JONES
A Test Case for Protection by the Mother Country   2

JOHN HAYS HAMMOND
Which Rider in the Saddle — Uitlander or Boer?   12

II. CAUSED BY CAPITALIST PROFITEERS?

JOHN. A. HOBSON
A Small Confederacy of International Mine-Owners   18

III. CAUSED BY JAMESON'S "CRIMINAL BLUNDER"?

R. C. K. ENSOR
Chamberlain Did Not Foreknow the Raid   26

ETHEL DRUS
British Officials Were Guilty   32

JEAN van der POEL
"Raking up the Raid"   36

IV. THE CLASH OF OPINION IN BRITAIN, 1899

E. T. COOK
A Far Ranging Boer Conspiracy   40

W. T. STEAD
How the British Government Caused the War   45

V. CAUSED BY JINGOISM?

JOHN. A. HOBSON
The Forces of Press, Platform, and Pulpit   49

VI. A WAR TO PRESERVE THE BRITISH EMPIRE?

R. C. K. ENSOR
The Whole Future of the Dominions Was Concerned   54

C. W. de KIEWIET
Britain's Goal — A United South Africa   58

WILLIAM L. LANGER
The Blunders of Imperial Diplomacy   60

**RONALD ROBINSON, JOHN GALLAGHER, AND
ALICE DENNY**
South Africa: Another Canada or Another United States?   70

J. S. MARAIS
The Threat of an Independent South Africa   79

VII. CAUSED BY PERSONALITIES?

J. L. GARVIN
Chamberlain — A Wise and Resourceful Statesman?   86

ALFRED MILNER
Reform in the Transvaal or War   95

Suggestions for Additional Reading   101

Introduction

THE Anglo-Boer War of 1899–1902 may not compare in magnitude with the two World Wars of this century, but it was, nonetheless, a sanguinary struggle which has been accorded a considerable significance by historians. The war marked, at least for Great Britain, the high tide of imperialist spirit which flowed during the 1890's. In tthe words of one writer, "it was in the South African question that the 'new or *fin de siècle* imperialism' found its fullest expression." [1]

Many historians have treated the war as a case study, one of the best examples of the way in which imperialist forces operated in actual practice — an example which frequently has a moral. Historians familiar with South Africa are concerned with the influence which the war may have had in molding the subsequent history of that area, and they raise the question of relationship between this struggle and the emergence of the Republic of South Africa in 1961. For most students the chief interest of the war lies in the sharp conflict of opinion in regard to causes, a conflict which has been waged ever since the months before the war began.

The readings in this book are selections from a number of the more significant historical writings on causes of the war which, taken together, constitute a problem in historical interpretation. Although a more complete picture may be found in the great body of historical literature now available, the readings here will enable the student to weigh the evidence for the various conflicting interpretations and to become, in a sense, "his own historian."

For Britain the last five years of the nineteenth century brought an upsurge in imperial enthusiasm never hitherto equalled and not subsequently maintained. These have been called the "braggart years," later viewed as "a lapse from accepted standards of British imperial morality." As a result of the war, Liberals and Radicals increased their opposition to aggressive imperialism, while after 1905 the public became increasingly absorbed with domestic problems and with the darkening skies on the European horizon. In recent years historical scholars have been conducting fresh studies of imperial thought in Britain during the nineteenth century, with the result that previously held interpretations are being modified. The "imperialist" school of thought in the latter part of the century is now regarded as having been less ardently expansionist than was formerly believed, and the "Little England" school as more concerned with liberalizing the Empire than with its liquidation. But there is no doubt that the advent of Joseph Chamberlain as Colonial Secretary in 1895 gave an immediate boost to the imperialist cause. He injected a new spirit into the whole range of imperial policy and ended the subordinate position hitherto assigned to colonial affairs. As the most dynamic figure in English political life during the next decade, Chamberlain devoted his great energy and ability to advancing the imperial ideal. He promoted federation and economic cooperation within the Empire. The Diamond Jubilee of 1897, with its pag-

---

[1] N. G. Garson, "British Imperialism and the Coming of the Anglo-Boer War," *The South African Journal of Economics,* XXX (June 1962), 140.

eantry of empire, symbolized the new temper. At the same time a rising wave of
international rivalry produced crises which
extended from the Far East to the tip of
Africa. The year 1898 witnessed a scramble
among the powers for concessions in China,
while in the Sudan the Fashoda crisis carried Britain and France to the verge of conflict. The year 1899 brought war in South
Africa.

Even with the hindsight of history, the
long-term effects of war are difficult to de-
termine with confidence, and the Anglo-
Boer War is no exception. It lasted for
more than two and one half years and resulted not only in heavy loss of life in the
two armies but also in systematic destruction of Boer homes and livestock, and, as
an indirect result of concentrating Boer
families in camps, the death of some 4,000
Boer women and 16,000 children. By a
generous peace (the Treaty of Vereeniging,
1902) the British government did much to
heal the scars. In 1906 the new Liberal
government, in a notable act of reconciliation, granted self-rule to the Transvaal and
the Orange Free State, and in 1909 these
recent enemy territories joined with other
colonies to form the Union of South Africa.
Former generals on the Boer side, such as
Louis Botha and Jan Christiaan Smuts, remained loyal to the British connection, and
South Africa entered both World Wars on
the side of Britain. A legacy of bitterness,
nevertheless, remained. One respected authority holds that "far from dooming the
national idea, the strain of war and shock
of defeat made the Afrikanders as a people." [2]

The controversy over causes of the war
has been wide-ranging and the conflicting
positions were staked out even before the
fighting began. Within Britain itself an
earnest and outspoken minority in 1899
criticized the war policy in penetrating
fashion. As time passed, each major view-

point of 1899 found its champions among
historians. During the nineteen-thirties
new and revealing materials were published, chiefly the *Milner Papers* and Mr.
J. L. Garvin's *Life of Joseph Chamberlain*.
But the most energetic and critical prob-
ing of the war's causes has occurred since
1945, stimulated by the availability of new
source materials, chiefly the papers of
Joseph Chamberlain and Cecil Rhodes, files
in the Public Records Office in London,
and the Bower and Innes papers in South
Africa. The new materials have prompted
a greatly intensified study of the background of the war and significant revisions
of interpretation.

Divergent interpretations confront the
student on almost every point related to
causes of the war. At first the question
may be: "Which side, Boer or British, was
primarily responsible for the conflict?" Or:
"Which leaders?" Soon the more challenging question will arise: "What caused the
war?" Was it the spirit of fair play arous-
ing Britons to protect their fellow nationals
against misrule and oppression? Was it the
capitalist mining interests in their search
for greater profits? Was it the spirit of Boer
nationalism, resolved to eliminate British
paramountcy and establish a South Africa
under Boer domination? Was it the sense
of imperial mission on the part of British
leaders, pushing for federation on the
Canadian model as the best long-term solution for South Africa? Was it the aggressive spirit of British imperialism driving to
consolidate power in South Africa? What
was the role of public opinion? Did an
aroused "jingoism" sweep the British government into a war policy against its better
judgment, or was "the great sleepy British
public" manipulated into war, unaware of
what the issues really were? The readings
in this book cover a fairly wide spectrum
of historical interpretation in regard to the
war. By examining the conflicting view-
points set forth since 1899 and the evidence in their support the student should,
hopefully, be able to formulate his own answers to the questions listed above.

[2] Eric A. Walker, "Lord Milner and South
Africa," *Proceedings of the British Academy,*
XXVIII (1942), 176.

What motives aroused the British public in 1899 to form ranks behind a policy of showdown with the Boers? To most persons the issues were twofold. The war was, first of all, a struggle for justice, a war to protect British subjects who were denied elementary rights by a backward and stubborn, even tyrannous regime. Second, the war was being fought to protect legitimate imperial interests against the aggressive regime of President Paul Kruger in the Transvaal; for two decades he had blocked federation in South Africa, built up powerful armaments, approached European powers for assistance, and threatened to unite the Dutch of all South Africa in a move to end Britain's paramount position there.

The obligation of a government to protect its citizens in their travel and business pursuits in foreign countries was then accepted in more unquestioned form than it is today. The doctrine expressed by Lord Palmerston in his famous "Civis Romanus sum" speech of 1850 had gained acceptance as "Civis Britannicus sum." The issue of Uitlander rights in the Transvaal and their protection by Britain is a main theme in the opening section, "A War to Protect British Subjects in the Transvaal." The student must consider several questions with regard to these rights. Just how intolerable were conditions for the rank and file? Was there a legal or moral obligation for the British government to intervene? What was the nature and purpose of Uitlander leadership? Was it in fact the Uitlander grievances which led to intervention by the British government?

The first reading is by Arthur Keppel-Jones, a Canadian historian who has written extensively on South African history. His account brings out the long background of friction between Boer and Briton, between the new industrial population in the Transvaal and "an antiquated and static rural society." Professor Keppel-Jones is restrained and objective, yet critical of the Boer regime: "the overthrow of the narrow oligarchy of the Republic was the essence of the solution." His emphasis differs from that in many other accounts in that he sees no conspiracy, either by capitalists or British officials, nor does he present the war as primarily a struggle for paramountcy between Britain and the South African Republic. He emphasizes rather the conflict between rival groups in the Transvaal, and he suggests that if the British government had refused to intervene it "might have cost her the loyalty of thousands of her own people" in the self-governing Empire, who looked upon this as a test case for the principle of protection by the Mother Country.

Vigorous support for the cause of Uitlander grievances is found in the second reading, taken from the *Autobiography* of John Hays Hammond, the American mining engineer. Hammond lived in the Transvaal during the years before 1896 as a mining specialist in the employ of Cecil Rhodes. He writes vividly of conditions in the Transvaal as seen by the Uitlanders and the mining interests.

A diametrically opposite point of view on these questions will be found in the third selection, by the brilliant English economist and journalist, J. A. Hobson. Hobson spent several months prior to the war travelling in South Africa. His book, *The War in South Africa, Its Causes and Effects* (1900), is the outstanding statement of the case for an economic interpretation of the war. He ridicules utterly the contention that rank and file grievances were either serious in themselves or even a main cause of British intervention. Instead, he pushes home the argument that a small group of moneyed interests, the mining capitalists and their financial allies, "engineered" the war by a campaign of trumped-up grievances which, in the end, drew the British government and public to their rescue. It was all done, says Hobson, for the sake of increased profits: "The mining capitalists stood to gain an income of two millions and a half by a successful political or military coup." Hobson's books and articles — for he was a prolific writer — had a great influence on subsequent interpretation of the war. The following statement by a recent writer is one among many examples of the Hobsonian view:

But who can really doubt that the simple issue on which the war was fought was whether or not independent Boer sovereignty was to be cleared out of the way of the British entrepreneurs and investors who wanted to make their fortunes out of mining the diamonds and gold which, it had been discovered, underlay the fields which the Boers were tilling? [3]

No consideration of the Anglo-Boer War can leave out of account the Jameson Raid, which began late in December, 1895, and ended disastrously four days later. Many historical accounts leave the impression that war was almost a foregone conclusion following this episode. Since about 1946 the Raid and its effects have undergone the most intensive re-examination by historians. New evidence has been sifted and detailed studies of the Raid have appeared. An immense amount of fine detective work has gone into the single key question as to whether the Colonial Secretary, Mr. Joseph Chamberlain, foreknew the Raid and whether he surreptitiously supported it, whether the Raid was a strictly private venture or whether it had British official sanction and assistance.

The extracts in this section present the conclusions of three historians. The first is by the British historian, R. C. K. Ensor. Ensor gives a circumstantial account of the Raid and the subsequent inquiry by a select committee of the House of Commons. On the vital question of official complicity he upholds essentially the view which was made official by the Inquiry of 1897, namely that Chamberlain had neither foreknowledge nor complicity. Quite opposite conclusions are set forth in the other two extracts. Miss Ethel Drus, a scholar whose experience stems both from South Africa and England, summarizes evidence brought to light since 1946, based partly on her own study of the Chamberlain papers and of official records, partly on the work of

[3] John Strachey, *The End of Empire* (London: Victor Gollancz, 1959), 91.

other scholars. The result is a strong cumulative case against Chamberlain. The third reading is from the book-length study by the South African historian, Dr. Jean van der Poel. Having set forth in detail the case against Chamberlain, Miss van der Poel, in her concluding chapter, argues the unfortunate effects of the subsequent "whitewashing" of Chamberlain by the Inquiry, and of his remaining in office.

During the 1890's Britons were by no means united in the cause of imperialism. The very enthusiasm for empire, long a target for radicals and many Liberals, made the cause increasingly suspect by the time of the Diamond Jubilee. An examination of periodical literature in the months before the war reveals how sharp the divergence of opinion really was. The extracts included under the heading "Conflict of Opinion in Britain, 1899," give the opposing views of two contemporary writers. The argument that for many years there had existed a Boer plan or "conspiracy" by Kruger and his clique to eliminate British power in South Africa was given wide publicity in 1899 and it gained increasing acceptance in Britain. With varying degrees of supporting evidence, the case was set forth in numerous articles and in some books. It received official sanction in the dispatches of the High Commissioner, Lord Milner. Documentary evidence of such a plot does not exist, but the circumstantial evidence was found convincing by many contemporaries and by not a few later historians. The first reading in this section is by the able London journalist and editor, Edward T. Cook, who states the case for Boer aggression. The second selection is by W. T. Stead, another distinguished journalist. He opposed the war in most uncompromising fashion and gained considerable unpopularity by charging that the nation had been cajoled and hoodwinked into war by the aggressive leadership of Milner and Chamberlain. Both these articles have found support in later interpretations by historians.

The spectrum of contemporary opinion

is completed by the reading on "jingoism." Here is another selection by the economist and critic, J. A. Hobson. Continuing his previous criticism of the war policy, Hobson published in 1901 a small book, *The Psychology of Jingoism,* in which he argued that Britain had been swept into war by "a collective or mob passion" engendered by a small group of known men and their supporters of "the press, the platform, and the pulpit. . . ." Contemporary periodical literature contains abundant examples of the "jingo" spirit which would lend support to Hobson's thesis.

All of the interpretations so far discussed have emphasized the idea of a war brought on by the interests of particular groups — whether Uitlanders, the capitalist mining interests, Boer nationalists, or imperial "jingoes." A broader interpretation, one which deemphasizes the special interest theory, is the view that considerations of imperial policy by the British government constituted the principal cause of war in 1899. Historians have assigned various motivations to the imperial policy; to some the motive stemmed from the prevailing mood of imperial aggrandizement; to others it was defense of the Empire against disruption from Boer nationalism; to still others it was the more idealistic motive of promoting federation on the Canadian model, for the good of South Africa as well as the Empire. Grouped under the heading "A War to Preserve the British Empire" are five readings, all differing in emphasis and all written since 1935.

First in this group is the account by the British historian R. C. K. Ensor. While admitting errors on the part of British leadership, Ensor sets forth strong arguments in support of the government's policy. He points to the menace from "a strong aggressive element" on the Boer side, along with Britain's reasons for expecting military victory, and her need to preserve the loyalty of her subjects in South Africa and in the Dominions. The second reading is by C. W. de Kiewiet, an American historian. In a passage notable for its lack of rancor

and the absence of named villains, de Kiewiet emphasizes the fact that for a generation the goal of British policy had been promotion of a federated and self-governing South Africa. He raises the question as to whether in 1899 one dissident community should any longer have been permitted to obstruct the unification which seemed destined for South Africa.

In sharp contrast to the preceding accounts is that by William L. Langer, another American historian. He presents an analysis of events between 1896 and 1899 which led to war, the focus falling on diplomatic negotiations more than on the motivations behind them, and, in the end, on the influential roles of Alfred Milner and Joseph Chamberlain. While Professor Langer's research was in progress, the *Milner Papers* were published and this enabled him to write the best-informed account of the High Commissioner's role which had appeared up to that time.

The fourth and fifth readings in this section, both of which were published in 1961, have much in common in their conclusions, although differing in approach and emphasis. The Cambridge University historians, Ronald Robinson and John Gallagher (with Alice Denny), examine Britain's role in Africa during the latter nineteenth century from the viewpoint of officials responsible for formulating policy. Basing their work largely on official documents and the personal papers of participants, the authors set forth the imperial reasoning which dictated major policy decisions. The work sheds significant light on factors which resulted in the Anglo-Boer war.

The final reading is by the South African historian, Professor J. S. Marais. Like the previous authors, Professor Marais emphasizes the question of motives behind British policy. Rejecting the thesis that capitalists or jingoes played the key role in 1899, Professor Marais views the war as resulting from a deliberate decision made by British leadership, a decision based on the recognition that a burgeoning South

African Republic was rapidly outstripping its colonial neighbors in economic growth and thus would become a magnet attracting not only South Africans of Dutch descent but also those of British or other descent into an independent "United States of South Africa." This factor, argues Marais, convinced the British government that an immediate assertion of imperial paramountcy was imperative. Afrikaner nationalism must be brought under control.

In his search for ultimate truth the historian often finds the question of motivation one of the most difficult problems. In the light of these five interpretations by competent historians, what really were the considerations which influenced the British government in 1899? How important were they in relation to factors previously discussed? And what judgment should the historian render on them today?

What was the role of leading personalities in bringing on the war? And what was the range of choice before them? Did fighting come as the result of a groundswell of underlying forces which the decisions of statesmen merely reflected, or did leading figures guide and control events, as well as public opinion? Controversy has long centered on Joseph Chamberlain and Alfred Milner. The widespread contemporary view that Chamberlain was largely responsible for the war crisis is illustrated by a cartoon printed in London in September, 1899, which shows a blindfolded John Bull at the edge of an abyss marked "WAR." Behind, and urging him forward, is the figure of the Colonial Secretary, with the words, "That's the way, Mr. Bull. Straight on!" On the other hand, publication of Milner's dispatches in the summer of 1899 convinced some persons, such as W. T. Stead, of Milner's primary role. The brother-in-law of A. J. Balfour, wrote at the time, "that if it was any man's war it was Milner's, and that Chamberlain only came second in responsibility through the fearlessness and 'pushfulness' with which he carried out the policy urged on

him by Milner." [4] What was the relationship between these men? Was either the agent or tool of the other, or did they have a near identity of views? Did Chamberlain push a reluctant cabinet and country into war, or is his biographer correct in stating that "he never failed in patience or diplomatic resource during these months"?

The first reading in the final section, "The Role of Personalities" is from Mr. J. L. Garvin's full-length *Life of Joseph Chamberlain.* His account sheds a great deal of light on the thought and role of the Colonial Secretary, whom he strongly defends. The second extract is from the *Milner Papers,* published in 1931 and now regarded as the best single source on the coming of war. These two readings will help recreate the atmosphere of 1899 on the official British side. They provide primary source material in the speeches of Chamberlain and the dispatches of Milner, and they will surely bring the student closer to reality in his judgment on men and events.

One of the challenging aspects of history is that it raises broader questions than "who?" or "what?"; historical study should lead to a better understanding of the factors which guide and shape human conduct. Is it true, for example, that historical events are basically determined by economic factors, or are the economic factors frequently subordinate? How important is the role of ideals, the striving for human betterment? How correct is it to speak of the "inevitability" of historical events? Was the Anglo-Boer War in fact an "irrepressible conflict," or did it result from human error? What part is played by the "climate of ideas" in any given period as a determinant of events? Is it really possible to draw lessons from the past? The problems of the Boer War may stimulate thought in regard to these questions.

[4] Eric Stokes, "Milnerism," *The Historical Journal,* V (1962), 53.

[NOTE: The footnotes which appeared in many of the original publications from which these readings were taken are not reproduced here.]

IDENTIFICATIONS OF PERSONS

Mentioned in the Readings

BALFOUR, ARTHUR JAMES, EARL OF, First Lord of the Treasury and Leader of the House of Commons, 1891–2 and 1895–1905; Prime Minister, 1902–5.

BEIT, ALFRED, mining magnate, friend and adviser of Cecil Rhodes.

BOTHA, GENERAL LOUIS, Commandant-General of Boer forces; Prime Minister of the Transvaal, 1907–10, and of the Union of South Africa, 1910–19.

BOWER, SIR GRAHAM, Imperial Secretary in South Africa, temp. Jameson Raid.

BUTLER, GENERAL SIR WILLIAM FRANCIS, acting High Commissioner in Milner's absence, 1898–9.

CAMPBELL-BANNERMAN, SIR HENRY, Liberal Party leader, 1898–1905; Prime Minister, 1905–8.

CHAMBERLAIN, JOSEPH, Unionist leader; Colonial Secretary, 1895–1903.

EDGAR, TOM, English workman shot by a Boer Policeman.

FAIRFIELD, EDWARD, Assistant Under-Secretary at the Colonial Office, temp. Jameson Raid.

FITZPATRICK, SIR PERCY, South African leader and author, secretary of the Reform Committee at Johannesburg, temp. Jameson Raid.

GREENE, SIR WILLIAM CONYNGHAM, British Agent at Pretoria, capital of the Transvaal.

GREY, ALBERT, EARL, a director of the British South African Company; agent of Cecil Rhodes prior to the Jameson Raid.

HAMMOND, JOHN HAYS, American-born mining engineer, a leading conspirator in the Jameson Raid.

HARCOURT, SIR WILLIAM VERNON, Liberal Party leader, 1896–8.

HARRIS, DR. FREDERICK RUTHERFOORD, Agent of Rhodes in planning the Jameson Raid.

HOFMEYR, JAN HENDRIK, leader of the Afrikaner Bond in Cape Colony.

JAMESON, DR. LEANDER STARR, leader of the Jameson Raid, Premier of Cape Colony, 1904–8.

JOUBERT, PETRUS JACOBUS, Commandant-General of Boer forces at the start of war.

KOTZÉ, SIR JOHN GILBERT, Chief Justice in the Transvaal, dismissed by President Kruger.

KRUGER, STEPHANUS JOHANNES PAULUS, President of the South African Republic (Transvaal), 1883–1902.

LEYDS, DR. WILLEM JOHANNES, Hollander State Secretary in the Transvaal; Minister Plenipotentiary in Europe, 1898–9.

MAGUIRE, ROCHFORT, agent of Rhodes in London, temp. Jameson Raid.

MILNER, SIR ALFRED, VISCOUNT, High Commissioner for South Africa, 1897–1905.

REITZ, FRANCIS WILLIAM, Ex-President of the Orange Free State who became State Secretary in the Transvaal, 1898.

RHODES, CECIL JOHN, financial magnate; Managing Director of the British South African Company; Premier of Cape Colony, 1890–6.

ROBINSON, SIR HERCULES, High Commissioner for South Africa, 1895–7; created Baron Rosmead, 1896.

ROSEBERRY, ARCHIBALD PRIMROSE, EARL OF, Liberal imperialist; Prime Minister 1894–5.

SALISBURY, ROBERT CECIL, MARQUESS OF, *Conservative leader; Prime Minister,
1885–6; 1886–92; 1895–1902.*

SCHREINER, WILLIAM PHILIP, *leader of the Bond-Moderate coalition, and Prime
Minister of Cape Colony, 1898–1900.*

SELBORNE, WILLIAM PALMER, EARL OF, *Under-Secretary of State for the Colonies,
1895–1900.*

SMUTS, JAN CHRISTIAAN, *Transvaal State Attorney, later General; Prime Minister
of the Union of South Africa, 1919–24 and 1939–48.*

STEYN, MARTHINUS THEUNIS, *President of the Orange Free State, signed treaty of
alliance with the Transvaal.*

VILLIERS, SIR JOHN HENRY DE, *Chief Justice in Cape Colony, a moderate in 1898–9.*

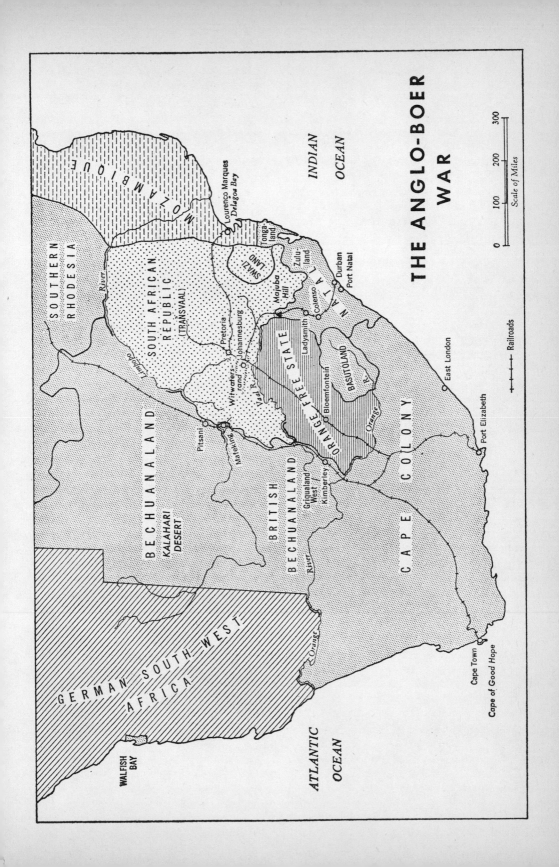

THE ANGLO-BOER WAR

The Conflict of Opinion

A War to Protect British Subjects?

"It must be borne in mind that the actions of the British government were being anxiously watched not only in the Cape Colony and Natal, but in Canada and Australasia. British colonists regarded this as a test case which would show whether their attachment to the Empire guaranteed to them the Mother Country's protection or not. . . ."

— ARTHUR KEPPEL-JONES

"The notion that Englishmen or white British subjects have commonly been made the victims of oppression and terrorism is grotesquely and utterly false. . . . On the contrary, Johannesburg was a place where liberty prevailed in its extremest form — with the single exception of the franchise."

— J. A. HOBSON

Caused by the Capitalist Mine-Owners?

"If this war can be successfully accomplished, and a 'settlement' satisfactory to the mine owners can be reached, the first fruits of victory will be represented in a large, cheap, submissive supply of black and white labour, attended by such other economies of 'costs' as will add millions per annum to the profits of the mines. It is no extravagance to argue that the blood and the money of the people of Great Britain are being spent for this purpose. . . ."

— J. A. HOBSON

Official Complicity in the Jameson Raid?

"The full text of the missing telegrams remains unpublished, but the quasi-incriminating passages in them can now be read. None suffices to rebut the otherwise overwhelming evidence that he [Chamberlain] did not foreknow the Raid."

— R. C. K. ENSOR

"Publication of concealed evidence could, however, only confirm what the available evidence has already put beyond doubt — that the Colonial Secretary and the High Commissioner were deeply implicated in the conspiracy that caused the Raid."

— JEAN VAN DER POEL

A Drive for Boer Paramountcy?

"The principle of Transvaal policy was . . . to become an absolutely independent and sovereign State, constantly enlarging its borders and throwing off daughter Republics; so that when the time came for the formation of the United South Africa aimed at by The Afrikander Bond, the paramount power should be that, not of Great Britain, but of the Dutch Republics."

— E. T. COOK

Caused by Jingoism?

"This conjunction of the forces of the press, the platform, and the pulpit, has succeeded in monopolizing the mind of the British public, and in imposing a policy calculated not to secure the interests of the British Empire, but to advance the private, political, and business interests of a small body of men. . . ."

— J. A. HOBSON

A War for the Empire?

". . . Kruger, even broken and in exile, lived till 1904; and if Great Britain had left her oppressed nationals unchampioned until then, she might by then have looked in vain for any loyal nationals in South Africa. . . . It concerned the whole future of the Dominions. . . ."

— R. C. K. ENSOR

"The Boer War was also the culmination of the British Government's lengthy quest for a united South Africa. . . . Where it was so clear that South Africa was naturally destined to unity, could a single community be allowed to deny that unity and to follow a course that made an unhappy separation the chief characteristic of political life?"

— C. W. DE KIEWIET

"The determination to forestall an independent United States of South Africa lies at the root of British policy. . . . The longer the South African Republic retained her independence the greater seemed the risk that the British colonies would be attracted away from the empire. . . . Afrikaner nationalism was the real enemy."

— J. S. MARAIS

Caused by Personalities?

"There is no doubt that opinion in the House of Commons is fluid, and on the whole, I think, bad. Perhaps they will rise to my fly — perhaps they won't."

— JOSEPH CHAMBERLAIN

"My view is, (1) that absolute downright determination plus a large temporary increase of force will ensure a climb down. It is 20 to 1. And (2) that, if it didn't and there was a fight, it would be better to fight now than 5 or 10 years hence. . . ."

— ALFRED MILNER

I. A WAR TO PROTECT
BRITISH SUBJECTS IN THE TRANSVAAL?

All accounts of conditions in the Transvaal agree on the reality of Uit-lander grievances, but there is wide disagreement on the extent to which the foreign element was denied basic rights and on whether British government intervention was justified. The first reading in this section is by Arthur Keppel-Jones, who is a specialist on South African history and Professor of History in Queen's University at Kingston, Ontario. His comprehensive account, without focusing on one cause alone, brings out the long background of friction between the two population groups and emphasizes the importance of the conflict between the Uitlanders and the Boer oligarchy.

The second reading is from the *Autobiography of John Hays Hammond*. Hammond had an adventurous and fascinating career. A graduate of Yale's Sheffield Scientific School, he became a mining specialist in the Far West, then went to South Africa in 1893 at $50,000 a year. Later he became chief consulting engineer of the Consolidated Gold Fields of South Africa, controlled by Rhodes. He was a principal conspirator in the plot which led to the Jameson Raid, as a result of which he was convicted of treason and sentenced to death; he was, however, released after five months in jail and payment of a $125,000 fine. He later became associated with the Guggenheim mining interests in the United States and became immensely wealthy. During the administration of President Taft he was a member of the inner White House circle. The account here is based on his experiences in the Transvaal. Due to limitations of space, his account of the Raid itself has been omitted.

A Test Case for Protection by the Mother Country

ARTHUR KEPPEL-JONES

In January, 1885, a conference was held at Fourteen Streams to discuss the Bechuanaland situation. President Kruger headed the Transvaal delegation. Cecil Rhodes was one of the British representatives. The "Colossus" and the "Lion of Rustenburg" faced each other for the first time.

So long as they lived, these two were to fight a duel which would be the dramatic expression of the whole political struggle of their age. Their personalities made so deep an impression on their followers that South African politics still tend to move along the lines which these men marked out. This has been a great misfortune. There were more beneficial forces at work than those which either of them represented. There were fundamental problems to be solved on which there was no great disagreement between Kruger and Rhodes and to which therefore their conflict made no contribution. Had Brand still been living in the 'nineties—he died in 1888—his influence would probably have changed the course of events immensely for the better. The rest of the story would have been more inspiring, too, if there had been a colossus in the party of Joubert, Schalk Burger, Esselen and Eugene Marais in the Transvaal, or among the Merrimans and Schreiners of the Cape. But these groups produced no one of the stature of Kruger and Rhodes.

Kruger was a product of the Trek and a descendant of trekkers and pastoralists. Rhodes, the son of a Hertfordshire parson, descended from a line of farmers. Both were men of inflexible will and determination. Each fought for the principle of nationality, British or Afrikaner. For that reason each is revered by later generations which cling to their national identity and traditions on either side. Yet neither can be regarded by a cool observer as a representative of the best traits in his national character.

In most ways they were in startling contrast. Kruger belonged to the Dopper Church, the most rigidly puritanical of Afrikaner sects; he regarded the singing of hymns as wicked levity. He was a Fundamentalist, sought his science in the Bible and believed the world was flat. He was at home in the world of cattle and big game and ox-wagons and farmhouses out of sight of their neighbours' smoke. Rhodes was a millionaire, a diamond magnate who controlled vast corporations with millions of capital. He dreamed of expanding British rule northwards right through the heart of Africa, of a railway from the Cape to Cairo, of consolidating the British Empire and linking it with the United States to dominate the world. He knew that money meant power. There were times when he seems to have thought there was nothing it could not do.

Both, therefore, had serious limitations. But they would not have won the devoted loyalty of thousands without other qualities. Both had great courage. Kruger, for all his puritanism, had a rugged and sometimes grim sense of humour. Rhodes had a gift of attracting not merely the friendship but even the love of men who knew him intimately. It can be said that he pursued wealth not for its own sake but for the political ends it would serve. His own personal tastes were simple. Yet money

From Arthur Keppel-Jones, *South Africa: A Short History*, 3rd revised edition (London, 1961), pp. 116–133. Reprinted by permission of Hutchinson and Co., Ltd.

corrupts. Neither Rhodes nor Kruger had a lofty or discriminating sense of honour. Yet both were great men. Kruger, himself a child of the Great Trek, personified the spirit of that movement, its strength as well as its weakness, its passion for freedom as well as its narrow isolationism. Rhodes not only gave to British South Africans an inspiring vision of their rôle in history, but, except for one short lapse, kept them consistently to the path of co-operation with their Afrikaner countrymen. His statesmanship rose far beyond the chauvinism which the Jameson Raid has caused to be associated with his name. His friendship with Hofmeyr was one of the great forces drawing the two nationalities together.

Rhodes had come to Natal in his youth to improve his health. The diamond fields soon attracted him and he made a fortune. That enabled him to go to Oxford for a pass degree; he attended to his mining interests at the same time as his studies. Returning to Kimberley, he found mining operations at a critical stage. So long as diamonds were to be scratched from the surface of the ground, every digger could attend to the few square feet of his own claim. But the busy throng on the surface disappeared from view as a great hole sank into the earth. Roadways between the claims fell in and the sides of the hole collapsed on to the diggers below. Claims had to be amalgamated. Rhodes proved his financial genius in his response to this challenge. He formed a company which controlled a whole mine; he defeated rival amalgamators and by 1890 his De Beers Consolidated Mines, Ltd., had united the whole of the South African diamond industry into one concern. Its property was worth £14,000,000 and it controlled the diamond market of the world. Big Business made its first appearance on the South African scene since the fall of the Dutch East India Company.

By that time Rhodes had used De Beers to promote the British South Africa Company, of which he was Managing Direc-

tor in South Africa. It received an imperial charter and became the means of colonising and conquering Rhodesia. That story lies outside the scope of this book, but it had repercussions on the countries to the south. The Pioneer Column entered Mashonaland in 1890; in the same year Rhodes became Prime Minister of the Cape.

He had, by then, his finger in another pie also. Since the days of the first diamond discoveries, gold was known to exist in the Transvaal. Mines were developed, principally in the eastern districts. In 1886 prospectors on the bleak uplands south of Pretoria, the Witwatersrand, discovered what proved to be the greatest goldfield in the world.

From Kimberley and elsewhere miners and financiers came to see. The galvanised iron shanties of the new mining camp of Johannesburg were the beginnings of a miraculous growth. Within a decade the town had 100,000 inhabitants. Along the line of reef, over a length of sixty miles, smaller towns grew up beside the mines. By 1895 it was known that this would not be an ephemeral gold-rush camp. The reef seemed inexhaustible and could be mined at deep levels. It had two distinguishing characteristics. The gold was very thinly distributed in the rock and it was very evenly distributed. There were no nuggets to make a digger rich overnight. The extraction was difficult and required expensive machinery. But since the reef was so uniform and reliable, and labour cheap, the investment of big capital in the mines, which the difficulties made necessary, was not unduly risky. The Rand was obviously a field for the experienced financiers of Kimberley.

Rhodes was one of these, but not the most important. His company, the Consolidated Goldfields of South Africa, gave him a share in the new wealth and a connection with Transvaal politics. But in Johannesburg even greater interests were represented by J. B. Robinson, Lionel Phillips, and others.

Rhodes was in a position which made it

almost if not quite impossible to reconcile his various duties and interests. He was responsible for the Cape government, De Beers, the Consolidated Goldfields, the Chartered Company and Rhodesia. As is the way with financial magnates, he used one of these rôles to ease his task in another.

His greatest single objective was the unification of South Africa under the British flag. Here he was following in the footsteps of Grey and Carnarvon. He rightly regarded the South African Republic as the chief obstacle in the way of this achievement. Kruger would have union on his own terms—the absorption of the rest of the sub-continent by his own state—but on no others. It was not for nothing that the Transvaal was called the South African Republic. The name was calculated, like that of the Soviet Union in later times, to smooth the way for the annexation of neighbouring states.

Before 1886 Kruger was in a poor bargaining position. He had even suggested a customs union with the Cape, a proposal which was turned down and was not to be repeated after the gold discoveries. Kruger, like every Transvaler since the days of Louis Trigardt, thought that the independence of his country would not be secure without a seaport of its own. The annexation of the New Republic, on the way to the sea, had been accompanied by a British annexation of Zululand. There still remained one small stretch of available coast—Tongaland, just south of the Portuguese border. Between this and the Transvaal High Veld lay the turbulent region of Swaziland, whose independence was guaranteed by the London Convention. Three times, between 1890 and 1895, Kruger negotiated with the British over Swaziland. The first time he had a good card to play. One of his burghers had got a concession from the Matabele Chief Lobengula. This came at the moment when Rhodes was preparing to send his Pioneer Column to Mashonaland on the strength of another of Lobengula's concessions. Kruger was pre-

pared to hold back his men at the Limpopo if he could have a *quid pro quo* on the east. What he got was a joint Anglo-Transvaal administration of Swaziland, and the right to a corridor to the sea, provided the Transvaal joined the Customs Union which the Cape and the Free State had just formed. The price was considered too heavy and the Volksraad never fulfilled the terms of this arrangement. When the republic was finally permitted to declare a protectorate over Swaziland, Kruger had just made a speech in which he announced that Germany could be called in to counterbalance British power in South Africa. Britain therefore annexed Tongaland and the Transvaal was finally cut off from the sea.

There could be no Transvaal port and no German port. The remaining alternative was Portuguese. Railway connection with Delagoa Bay would free the republic from dependence on British colonial ports. Even in the days of President Burgers this railway had been a favourite republican scheme. The presence of the tsetse fly in the low country made ox-wagon traffic to Lourenço Marques impossible. But the funds for a railway could never be raised before gold came to strengthen Transvaal credit. Then the Dutch and German financiers came forward with alacrity.

The Netherlands South African Railway Company, which was given a monopoly of Transvaal railway connections with other states, was floated in Holland. Dutch subscribers provided 29 per cent of the capital but kept to themselves more than two-thirds of the voting power. A greater number of shares was held by the republic itself, and a much greater number in Germany.

Kruger did what he could to prevent the Cape and Natal railways crossing his border before the Delagoa Bay line was completed. Long before any through connection was established it was necessary to build a line along the Rand to link the mines with their source of coal at Springs. The Railway Company was later able to boast that the traffic on this short line paid the interest on the construction of its whole system. In return for a railway loan Kruger allowed the main line from Port Elizabeth, which ran through the Free State to Viljoen's Drift, to be continued to the Rand. This was in 1892. It was not till two and three years later that the connections with Delagoa Bay and Natal were complete.

The railway company was the object of bitter attacks, and not only by the mining magnates. It was complained that construction was three times as expensive as it need have been; that the company provided "jobs for pals" and lucrative contracts for subsidiaries; that the Komati bridge, in the midst of country abounding in stone, was made of stone imported from Holland — of all countries! The company's profits were greater than its working expenses, and its dividends ten per cent and more. It was allowed to collect the customs duties on the Portuguese border and keep them for itself.

Recent investigations have taken much of the sting out of these and other charges. The construction of the line through difficult and unhealthy country from Komatipoort to the High Veld was necessarily expensive, and it was this line that Kruger very naturally regarded as a political necessity. The capital was difficult to raise in Europe; most of it had to be loan and not share capital, and the profits on the Rand line had necessarily to compensate for the expense of the route to Delagoa Bay. As for the Komati bridge, the local stone was unsuitable and the means to work it were lacking on the spot. Nor could personnel be recruited locally. The collection of customs duties was a consequence of the republic's guarantee of minimum profits to the company.

From the point of view of the foreign population on the Rand, these considerations were irrelevant. If the Cape Government Railways could provide, for whatever reasons, cheaper communication with the outside world, the Rand consumers saw no necessity for the Netherlands Company at all. Its tariffs were much heavier than those on the Cape railways. The latter cut their rates so as to capture the Rand traffic. It became cheaper to bring goods from the Cape to the Rand than over the much shorter line from Lourenço Marques. The company, to keep the traffic to its own routes, therefore trebled the rates on its short line from the Free State border to Johannesburg. The people concerned tried to escape this charge by unloading goods at Viljoen's Drift, on the Free State side of the Vaal, and bringing them to the Rand by wagon. Kruger then closed the drifts (fords) over the river to this traffic. But he had gone too far. A firm stand by the British government made him retreat. And he had united the Free Staters, the Cape Colonists (Dutch and English) and Great Britain against him.

There were many grounds besides its railway policy on which the Transvaal régime could be criticised. Monopolies were granted to favoured people. The dynamite monopoly, of vital concern to the mines, caused the price of dynamite to be three times as high as it would have been with free importation. This monopoly cost the mines £600,000 a year. Legal quibbles were used to deprive the mining companies of property and bring profit to officials and their friends. Eugene Marais, editor of *Land en Volk,* regularly exposed cases of bribery and challenged the people he named to sue him for libel. They never did so with success. One member of the Executive, who had supported the dynamite concession, was said to draw £10,000 a year from it thereafter for his pains. In connection with the Selati railway concession bribes were distributed to officials and legislators, and the President said he saw no harm in it.

Laws were passed with retroactive effect. When a Field-Cornet was convicted of ill-treating a Native the government paid his fine. Taxes were specially devised to fall mainly upon the Uitlander (foreign) population, which claimed that it contributed at least nine-tenths of the public revenue. In the critical years before the Boer War the Chief Justice claimed the right to test the constitutionality of laws, and for this he was dismissed.

The Uitlanders thus had serious grievances. They hoped to qualify for Transvaal citizenship and elect representatives who would redress them. The frustration of this hope produced the greatest grievance of all. It had formerly been very easy to become a burgher in the Transvaal, as it continued to be in the Free State. But the sudden influx of a large alien population produced a change. The naturalisation and franchise laws were tightened up. Petitions by many thousands of people, asking for easier terms, were treated with scorn and derision by President and Volksraad. One legislator challenged the foreigners to fight for the vote. At last it became impossible for an immigrant to get it till he had been fourteen years in the republic, twelve years a naturalised subject (having lost his previous nationality) and at least forty years old; and even then he would not vote in presidential elections. In effect, citizenship was impossible to acquire, though the government could always grant it to any favoured person.

Most of the aliens were British subjects, though there were many Germans and Americans. Of the British, a good many came from the Cape Colony and Natal. These felt their exclusion from political rights much more bitterly than the others. The great capitalists "did not care a fig for the franchise" (they preferred working with "electoral funds"), but the bulk of the immigrants, intending to make permanent homes on the Rand, were very serious in demanding it. Moreover, while denied the rights of citizenship, they were expected to shoulder its obligations. When some of them, called up for military service, refused to go, this was treated as evidence of their unfitness for the franchise.

Now consider Kruger's case. His people had won the Transvaal with blood and tears. They had moved great distances and made great sacrifices to find a country where they could be themselves and preserve their way of life. Now they were suddenly invaded by a horde of cosmopolitan fortune-seekers whose outlook and civilisation were poles apart from their own. In a few years the newcomers outnumbered the old burghers by two to one. If he gave them the vote, Kruger said, he might as well haul down the republican *Vierkleur*.

One of the Uitlanders' demands was for state support for English-medium schools. This was an inconsiderate demand, since the preservation of the Dutch character of the state was a fundamental condition of its existence. It was reasonable to expect new citizens to conform to this character. As for paying nine-tenths of the taxes and having no representatives, Kruger's attitude was bluff and logical: if they didn't like it, they could go. If they stayed, he might take that as a sign that they were doing well enough.

The mining companies were not doing badly, but it must be remembered that the really significant grievances were those of the rank and file of the Uitlander population. These formed the Transvaal National Union to demand redress of all their grievances. It is significant that the successive chairmen of this Union were South Africans by birth. So had Arnot, Shepstone and many other leading "imperialists" been. Of the Englishmen who played political parts in South Africa, those most responsible for British expansion and a firm line with the republics were commonly men who closely identified themselves with the British colonists. The struggle was as much between rival groups in South Africa itself, as between the Afrikaners and the British government.

The demands of the National Union fell on deaf ears. Feelings were embittered by folly on both sides. The republican flag was torn down and trampled on by a Johannesburg mob. Kruger spoke of the Uitlanders in rough and sometimes unprintable terms. "Go back and tell your people," he said to a deputation, "I shall never give them anything: I shall never change my policy, and now let the storm burst."

It did. The National Union began to organise a revolution, and Rhodes took a hand in it; partly, it has been said, because he was disappointed in his hopes of a "New Rand" in Rhodesia, and wanted to bend the old Rand to his purposes. Many successful revolutions have had less justification than this one. Though the old Boer patriarchs, struggling to preserve what was dear to them, may win our sympathy, their case was weak. The wise conservative achieves something by making concessions to the spirit and needs of a new time. The late nineteenth century was not a time in which two-thirds of the people of a country (not counting Natives, whom all disregarded), paying nine-tenths of its taxes and owning a third of its land, could be kept indefinitely in a state of subjection. When it is remembered that the rulers were a simple people unversed in the ways of the world, and that the subjects could enlist the support of what was still the greatest of the Great Powers, Kruger's obstinacy seems still more foolish. If he were to preserve the old Transvaal unchanged, his only logical course was to follow the methods of Afghanistan or old Japan. He should have put up a notice at the Vaal River like that on the Khyber Pass, which says, "It is absolutely forbidden to cross this frontier." But the London Convention forbade this; and if it had been done, the state revenue would not have multiplied twenty times in ten years.

Plotting therefore began in Johannesburg. Rifles and machine-guns were smuggled in under loads of coke or concealed in oil-drums with oil dripping deceptively from the taps. Most of these loads came from the sidings of De Beers Consolidated at Kimberley. There was a plan to seize the arsenal in Pretoria. Would the revolution be a purely domestic one, or carried out under the British banner, with a demand for British annexation? The plotters were so divided on this point that at the last moment they postponed "flotation of company", as it was called in their cryptic telegrams, and the movement seemed to have fizzled out. Quite apart from divisions in the ranks of the "shareholders," they had not nearly enough arms or ammunition for their purpose.

But on the hot afternoon of December 30, 1895, when the leading conspirators were gathered together, they received a telegram which made their blood run cold. It read: "The contractor has started on the earthworks with seven hundred boys; hopes to reach terminus on Wednesday." Thus was announced a "flotation" for which the subscribers wanted no responsibility and which would bring some of them within sight of the gallows.

The contractor was Dr. Jameson, intimate friend of Rhodes and Administrator of Rhodesia. He had been brought into the conspiracy because it was thought necessary to have support from outside the Transvaal to make sure of success. The Chartered Company was then building a railway from Mafeking to Bulawayo. On this excuse Rhodes got the Colonial Office to transfer to the Company's administration a "railway strip" through the Bechuanaland Protectorate. Down this strip Jameson brought a force of Mashonaland Mounted Police, and encamped them at a spot on the Transvaal border not far north of Mafeking. It was, of course, for this purpose that the Company had acquired the conveniently placed railway strip.

Rhodes and the Johannesburg plotters had provided this force in order to give outside support if anything should go wrong with the revolution. Jameson was given an undated letter from the leaders in Johannesburg calling him to come in to save their women and children from the Boers. When it appeared that the revolutionaries were divided in their aims and insufficiently armed, they sent two messengers as well as telegrams to Jameson to "postpone flotation." All the messages reached him. Rhodes, too, tried to stop him, though his telegram arrived too late. But Rhodes had once said to another officer: "You cannot expect a Prime Minister to write down that you are to seize ports, etc. But when he gives you orders to the contrary, *disobey them.*" He reaped the bitter fruit of this seed when Jameson disobeyed the explicit orders reaching him from all sides.

Two years earlier, Jameson had fought a war with the Matabele and added their territory to that of Mashonaland. Because of the new weapon, the machine-gun, the war was a walk-over. Jameson became too confident. He had, too, been reading Macaulay's essay on Clive. "You may say what you like," he said, "but Clive would have done it."

Fortified by these thoughts he led his band across the Transvaal border and made a dash for Johannesburg. The Boers were quite capable of handling this sort of situation. Their Commandos assembled with great speed and stood between the invader and his goal. The High Commissioner, on hearing the news, repudiated Jameson's action and sent a messenger to order him back. The order was disobeyed. On the fourth day Jameson was trapped. When further resistance was hopeless, a white apron was seized from a Native woman and hoisted in sign of surrender. The same night the invaders were all lodged in Pretoria gaol.

De Kiewiet says of the Raid that "it was inexcusable in its folly and unforgivable in its consequences." No one would now question this judgment. The folly was so great as to be almost unbelievable. A British force, operating from British territory, invaded a country with which the Queen was at peace. It did not do so in sufficient strength to have any chance of success. The Raid was supposed to assist a revolution organised in Johannesburg, yet the revolutionaries had given Jameson the most emphatic orders not to move.

It was pointed out at the time that the Transvalers under Pretorius had conducted an almost exactly analogous raid into the Free State in 1857. Kruger had been one of the invaders, though he had not approved of the policy. He used his influence to avert hostilities and cause a withdrawal of the Transvalers. The analogy is

significant, but it does not excuse Jameson's crime.

The leaders of the movement in Johannesburg were compromised. Sixty-four of them were arrested. Of these, four were condemned to death. But although a patriot chose this moment to bring from Somerset East to Pretoria no less an historical relic than the beam from which the Slagter's Nek rebels had been hanged, the penalty was commuted to a fine of £25,000 each. Rhodes and his friend Beit paid on behalf of the prisoners. The others were punished by imprisonment for which also a fine was substituted. With great wisdom Kruger handed Jameson and his raiders over to the British Government for trial. They got very light sentences.

A committee of the House of Commons and another of the Cape House of Assembly enquired into the responsibility for the Raid. Some members of the London Committee believed that Joseph Chamberlain, then Colonial Secretary, was implicated, but they failed to prove it. Subsequent evidence has shown that he knew of the contemplated rising and did not discourage it. He certainly knew nothing about the Raid. So the blame must fall mainly on Rhodes. He encouraged and financed the movement, yet failed to control the people he had stirred up. He had so often supported irregular political and military proceedings that Jameson might naturally suppose he would support this one.

Of the consequences of the Raid, direct and indirect, we have not yet seen the end. The immediate results were serious enough. The Kaiser sent Kruger a congratulatory telegram which began the estrangement of Britain from Germany. Rhodes parted company from Hofmeyr and most of his Afrikaner friends (this was a revolution in Cape politics), resigned his Premiership and his seat on the board of the Chartered Company. A stop-gap ministry took office in the Cape Colony, where Briton and Afrikaner drew apart in hatred and suspicion. Many of the British colonists, of whom Merriman was the outstanding representative, felt that their flag had been besmirched by the underhand dealings of Rhodes and Jameson. Others thought that the Uitlanders on the Rand, by failing to rise, had betrayed Jameson and his brave boys. J. C. Smuts, a young Cape advocate just back from Cambridge, abandoned his British nationality in disgust and settled in the Transvaal, where he was soon to become State Attorney. The Free State turned its back on the Cape and formed a defensive alliance with its republican neighbour. Up in Rhodesia the Matabele, followed by the Mashona, took advantage of the absence of the police to rise in rebellion. Rhodes himself played a brave and dramatic part in the pacification. In the Transvaal there had been, among the old burghers themselves, considerable opposition to Kruger. This was now almost silenced, and the president was re-elected for a fourth term in 1898. For a century there had been suspicion of British motives and fear of British treachery. The suspicion and fear seemed now to be confirmed beyond a shadow of doubt, and all the earlier policies of Britain were thrown into darker relief. Even Natal drew apart from the Cape. The Garden Colony had received responsible government in 1893, and now wished to take advantage of its low customs tariff to trade with the Transvaal. Throughout South Africa there were fear, bitterness, recrimination and broken friendships.

What did the future hold? In less than four years from the Raid the British Empire and the Republics were at war. One asks whether the war was inevitable. Underlying its immediate occasions there appeared to be a fundamental antagonism. There were some resemblances to the Civil War in America. Britain, like the American Union, represented a modern industrial civilisation; the republics, like the Confederacy, an antiquated and static rural society. Was there an "irrepressible conflict" between them? The American conflict came because both sides shared a common country, and the national policy had to take one line or another. But South Africa was not one country. Could the separate parts not agree to differ? They could not, because the conflict was not in essence a difference of policy between different states; it was a struggle for supremacy within one state. The conflict was irrepressible; but that is not to say that it had inevitably to be resolved by war.

Within the Transvaal two different civilisations came to grips. Their quarrels related to every aspect of the state's affairs: taxation, railway and customs policies, monopolies, police, the administration of justice, the method of legislation, the official language, education. There can be no doubt that the Uitlanders, if enfranchised, would never have been content till these questions were settled to their own satisfaction. Such a change would have destroyed the republic of the Boers, whether the Vierkleur continued to wave or not. Therefore the old burghers were determined to prevent it. Their attitude was as natural as that of their opponents; but which side was right? The best answer is perhaps that the Boers were supported by the letter of the law, but the Uitlanders by the principles of historical development and by every historical analogy.

It was assumed that Kruger would not make any concessions on the mere demand of the Uitlanders. "I shall never give them anything." Most of them, being British subjects, then naturally turned to Britain for assistance. Had Britain either the right or the duty to interfere? Her right to do so depended partly on the articles of 1884, partly on the disputed "suzerainty." But the articles of the Convention did not cover the case, and nobody could say what suzerainty meant. The problem seemed insoluble in theory; but in April, 1899, it became a question of practical politics, and a solution had to be found. Some 20,000 Uitlanders petitioned the Queen for protection. It must be borne in mind that the actions of the British government were being anxiously watched not only in the Cape Colony and Natal, but in Canada and Australasia. British colonists regarded this as a test case which would show whether their attachment to the Empire guaranteed to them the Mother Country's protection or not; whether Palmerston's *Civis Britannicus sum* was a sham or a reality.

As a matter of practical politics, Britain's disregard of the Uitlanders' petition might have cost her the loyalty of thousands of her own people; so that Kruger would have had it both ways. On the moral side there is a point of vital importance to be remembered. Up to August, 1899, every Transvaal proposal on the subject of the franchise contained a curious provision. There was to be a long interval between the Uitlander's naturalisation and his getting the right to vote. During this time — it was twelve years by the existing law — he could have no voice in the affairs of his adopted country and would have cut himself off from the country of his birth. Had it not been for this circumstance the Uitlander might have chosen one allegiance or the other and been expected to abide by his decision. But in fact there were no alternatives: he must be protected by his native country or not at all. World opinion today would not admit that a law-abiding person ought to renounce the privileges of one nationality without gaining those of another; nor did this seem right in 1899.

Chamberlain therefore took up the cudgels for the Uitlanders. A new High Commissioner, Sir Alfred Milner, took the initiative appropriate to the "man on the spot," but worked in harmony with the Colonial Secretary. Milner believed that, as long as it remained united, the British Empire was the mainstay of peace and freedom in the world, and that South Africa was a vital link in the chain that held it together. That meant that the British and those Afrikaners who were willing to share this allegiance to the Crown must be the dominant element in South Africa, not Kruger's republicans. For the task in hand he had all the qualities of a first-rate civil servant, but by temperament and training he was more an administrator than a diplomatist. But, since neither he nor Chamberlain

thought war to be inevitable at this stage, they had agreed to make the most of diplomacy first. Their principal aim was to get a reasonable franchise for the Uitlanders, after which Britain would accept no further responsibility for them. Milner met Kruger at the Bloemfontein Conference and this question was stiffly discussed. No agreement was reached.

In the Transvaal an important change of personnel had taken place. Several of the Hollanders whom Kruger had placed in the highest executive posts were removed and their places taken by Afrikaners. J. C. Smuts, the young advocate from the Cape Colony, became State Attorney, and F. W. Reitz, ex-President of the Free State, became State Secretary. These men brought a more realistic and progressive spirit into the negotiations, and they were helped by outside influences that were brought to bear on the President. Sir Henry de Villiers and J. H. Hofmeyr came up from the Cape to counsel moderation. The result was a change in Transvaal policy which put a very different complexion on the whole dispute.

A new dispatch from Reitz offered a five years' franchise which was to be retrospective; the price demanded was the tacit abandonment of the British claim to suzerainty, and no further interference in the internal affairs of the republic. Any remaining points in dispute could be settled by arbitration in which the Transvaal would not ask that foreign Powers should take part. Chamberlain saw several snags in this offer. The South African Republic had often repealed laws by the simple process of a resolution passed by the Volksraad at a single sitting. And its previous franchise laws and proposals had been hedged about by administrative complications which took back with one hand what had been given with the other. Britain could not pay the price asked unless the concession were to be effective and permanent. But Chamberlain's despatch, which he afterwards described as a "qualified acceptance," was so tactlessly and obscurely worded as to make it seem like a refusal. The Transvaal thereupon withdrew its offer. If the despatch had been worded as a clear acceptance, and the necessary qualifications tactfully introduced, there might have been no war. Chamberlain had had the power to prevent it. Kruger's régime would have been undermined from within, but that would have worried nobody but his own clique.

This possibility was even closer to the Uitlanders' grasp before the Raid. At that time most of South Africa was hostile to Kruger. Had the Uitlanders waited, and Jameson never left Rhodesia, Kruger was likely to lose the next presidential election as well as control of the Volksraad. The margin would not have been great, but the victors would have regarded Kruger's party as their main enemy, and this would have been a strong inducement to add Uitlanders to the electorate. After the Raid even the "liberal" Boer leaders, Joubert and Burger, were very chary of concessions. In 1895, and again in August, 1899, there was a prospect of a peaceful solution. But it must be repeated that the overthrow of the narrow oligarchy of the republic was the essence of that solution. Given the forces that were at work, the old régime could never have survived in peace. But its overthrow by peaceful means would have had very different results from its going down in a blaze of patriotic glory before superior force.

After the misunderstanding of August the continued interchange of despatches served little purpose. Both sides had to prepare for the possibility of a breakdown.

Milner had ceased to believe in the possibility of peace; and, since he thought that war would bring about the unification of all South Africa under the British flag, he was ready to face it. Maybe his full, clearly argued despatches stiffened Chamberlain. But several Boer writers have believed that Kruger's intransigeance was also to blame. "The only *casus belli*," Lord Bryce wrote, "has been the conduct of the two contending parties during a negotiation, the professed subject of which was in no sense a *casus belli*." In the end the guns went off almost of themselves.

Kruger had been buying German artillery and building fortifications ever since the Raid. Britain now ordered troops from India and the Mediterranean to Durban, and prepared to despatch an army corps. Republican commandos assembled on the Natal border, within sight of Majuba. British troops were held back from the borders, but the shadow of that mountain still fell across the whole British army.

If there was to be war, the only chance for the republics — the Free State stood by her ally — was to start it before the British forces had arrived in strength. Reitz therefore despatched an ultimatum: all troops on the borders of the republic to be withdrawn; troops that had arrived in South Africa since June 1 to leave the country; troops now on the high seas not to land. Chamberlain replied that the conditions "are such as Her Majesty's Government deem it impossible to discuss." On October 11 the Boer War — to the Boers the Second Freedom War — began.

Which Rider in the Saddle — Uitlander or Boer?

JOHN HAYS HAMMOND

THE most dramatic and critical period of my life was ushered in by the autumn of 1895. Two years had passed since my arrival in South Africa. Six months of that time I had spent with Barnato, two months on the trip to Mashonaland with Rhodes. In addition, I had made a visit to London and had been to Groote Schuur for an occasional conference with Rhodes. The major part of my attention, however, had been directed towards the management of the Consolidated Gold Fields Company, and I was particularly concerned with the technical details of the new deep-level mines.

Little of my time had been devoted to politics. I had listened to the discussions going on about me and had quickly become cognizant of the Uitlander grievances — they were the inevitable topic of conversation at every dinner table. I was sympathetic, of course, but not actively interested.

On many occasions I did go so far as to say that the law-abiding miners from England were enduring ill-treatment from Kruger's government that the men I had known out West in America would never have tolerated.

Only when the Boer policy directly affected the running of the mines under my management was I forced into political opposition. It became gradually obvious to me that if the Boer policy were not radically changed a conflict was inevitable.

About this time General "Slim" (Sly) Piet Joubert, later commander of the Transvaal forces in the Boer War, put the problem to me nicely.

"There are two riders but only one horse in the Transvaal," he said. "The question is, which rider is going to sit in front — the Uitlander or the Boer?"

"General," I replied, "we Uitlanders are paying nine-tenths of the cost of the horse and nine-tenths of his upkeep as well. I think we ought to be in the saddle."

Joubert shook his head gloomily and turned away. As the leader of the liberal party among the Boers, he meant well towards the Uitlanders, but his sympathies were not strong enough to carry him to the point of acting directly against the Kruger faction. Nevertheless, he had summed up the situation concisely: two opposite ideals were confronting each other.

Before the Jameson Raid the Boers were by no means united behind Kruger. From many talks I gained the impression that the younger Boers, at least, thought reform essential. Deputations of prominent young Boers had on various occasions warned Kruger that their understanding of the justice of the Uitlander position was such that they could take no active part in any trouble that might come up in Johannesburg.

In the liberal party, led by General Joubert, were Louis Botha and many others who attained political distinction during and after the Boer War. There was little love lost between the Kruger and Joubert parties; indeed, the controversies sometimes waxed intense.

Many of the Boers themselves alleged that, at the presidential election of 1888, Joubert had lost the presidency only because of Kruger's lavish and unscrupulous use of the state's money at the polls. Moreover, Kruger's illegal ousting of Joubert supporters from the Volksraad was common knowledge.

The Joubert faction did not agree with Kruger's conviction that the Uitlander was fit only for plundering. Chief Justice Kotzé, himself a nonpartisan, told the burghers in October, 1894, that "No one . . . will deny that the country is at present in a very critical position. . . . It depends entirely upon the people whether the impending change is to take place peaceably or to be accompanied by violence."

The Boer liberals (as well as the Uitlanders) had definite grievances. They vigorously objected to the swarms of Hollanders and Germans who were pouring into the country and filling the lucrative offices. Governmental expenditures had been augmented from about $750,000 in 1886 to upwards of $18,500,000 in 1896. The salaries paid in 1896 amounted to about $150 per head per annum for the total male Boer population. In defense of their position, the Kruger followers ascribed the protests of their political opponents to the younger and more liberal Boers' exclusion from these perquisites of office.

*   *   *

The government of the Transvaal was in the hands of Stephanus Johannes Paulus Kruger, known to his own people and to the world as Oom, or Uncle, Paul.

He had been president of the South African Republic, commonly known as the Transvaal, since 1883 and there was every probability that he would remain in office indefinitely. Nothing short of an internal revolution or the impairment of his faculties seemed likely to shake off his control over what was a mere simulacrum of a republic, inasmuch as it did not derive its just powers from the consent of the governed.

From Kruger's birth in Cape Colony in 1825 to his death in exile in 1904 his life was full of adventure. He had shared the hardships and dangers of his parents in the Great Trek. His education had been derived not from books, but from trekking, fighting, and hunting on the frontier. One could readily believe the many tales of his courage. The story of how, his thumb having been badly wounded, he himself cut it off with his knife had become a household legend.

I met Kruger first in 1893 in connection with the revision of the mining laws of the Transvaal. He was then sixty-eight years old. His massive frame still showed evidences of that brute physical strength which had become proverbial. A huge nose, a large firm mouth, keen eyes partially obscured by swollen lids, were set in a heavy, rugged face surrounded by a ragged fringe of beard. His forehead sloped back to where the long grizzled hair swept up in a defiant mane. In spite of his dignity of bearing, the impression I received was one of cunning rather than of intelligence.

He lived in an unpretentious one-story wooden building where he was frequently seen on the small front piazza, puffing at his pipe of strong Boer tobacco. He received me in the parlor which was fitted out in typical mid-Victorian style with horsehair furniture, and artificial flowers under glass globes. A marble-topped center table held bulky volumes among which was prominently displayed a Bible bound in pressed leather and titled in large gilt letters.

Oom Paul's religion had a decided touch of the fanatical. He belonged to the narrow and uncompromising Dopper sect of the Dutch Reformed Church. His speeches were peppered with Biblical quotations. He was a fundamentalist in every sense of the word. To him the first book of the Bible was literally true.

He even firmly believed that the world was flat. The stubbornness of this belief is illustrated by an anecdote told me by Captain Joshua Slocum, an American who visited Kruger while circumnavigating the globe in a thirty-foot sailing boat.

At the end of a short but pleasant interview in Pretoria, Oom Paul asked him, "In what direction, Captain, do you intend to continue your voyage?"

"I'm going right around the world, Mr. President," replied the captain.

"Don't lie," warned Kruger in all seriousness. "You mean across the world."

Kruger was born out of his time. He might have been a great leader, given a patriarchal society; there was no niche in the Twentieth Century Hall of Fame for a shepherd peasant leader. His very greed for land, and more land, for his burghers was against him. He wanted a succession of Dutch farms, each to include thousands of acres: he wanted Zululand, Bechuanaland, Matabeleland, Mashonaland, Swaziland, Stellaland, and a road to the sea. By devious methods he played one faction against another in his endeavor to attain these ends.

On the one hand was a simple, patriarchal, pastoral society; on the other, an urban industrial civilization. The reason for this schism between the Uitlander and the Boer of the Kruger type was not hard, therefore, to comprehend. The Boer burgher was in no way interested in mining; he was a peasant with the conservative, reactionary, and suspicious nature of that class. But he was more than this: he was cunning, brave, and stubbornly intent on keeping what he regarded as his birthright.

Those who possess a country invariably hate the invader. The question is often asked, "Why did the Uitlanders go to the Transvaal, if they were not wanted?" The answer is, they were wanted. With this in mind Kruger, in 1884, asked foreign capital, by a formal invitation in the London press, to come in and develop the mineral resources of his country. In return, he promised investors protection for their interests and a fair share of influence in the government. English investors, particularly, were attracted in answer to his invitation. The resulting activity of the Uitlander led within two years to the discovery of the famous gold deposits of the Witwatersrand near Johannesburg.

*   *   *

Rhodes had become to Oom Paul the epitome of all things he hated and distrusted. Again and again Rhodes tried to deal with Kruger. Even on the return from our Matabeleland trip in 1894, he stopped at Pretoria in a final effort to come to some sort of understanding as to the future of South Africa. Both men wanted a united country, but each for his own purposes and for his own people. The interview resulted in an impasse. This obstinate and obdurate Boer was virtually the only man Rhodes was never able to win over.

Kruger's personal detestation of Rhodes was extended to include almost all Uitlanders. His suspicion of us and of our motives was proof against all our attempts to attain what we considered our rights. He listened to the respectful petitions of the Uitlanders with grunted "Ja's," pulled at his pipe, and spat. Our spokesmen went away with the feeling that they had been talking to a stone wall — so impassive, so unimpressed, so adamant was he to all appeal of reason.

The effect of this uncompromising attitude was to unite the Uitlanders against a foe which threatened us all. In reality, we Uitlanders had little in common; not only were we of different races and languages, but so long as we were allowed social, political, and economic justice, it seemed of slight importance to us at that time whether the Vierkleur or the Union Jack waved over Johannesburg.

*   *   *

It was the sum total of various irritations that fired the mounting hostilities. Some individuals were activated by one set of grievances, some by another. For example, there was the question of education. Out of $310,000 allotted to Johannesburg for this purpose, less than $4000 was used for the Uitlander children, although they greatly outnumbered the Boer children and the Uitlander parents supplied the money to build and support the schools. Moreover, English was not taught in the schools. The Uitlander children had to learn Taal, the debased form of Dutch used by the Boers.

One of the most outrageous grievances was the Boer assertion of their right to draft Uitlanders for service in the native wars. More than a hundred English subjects were commandeered by the Boers for their expedition against the native chieftain Malaboch, and compelled to provide their own horses and arms. The five men who refused to obey the summons were imprisoned.

*   *   *

The unequal administration of justice touched the community even more closely than the commandeering of Uitlanders. No Uitlander was assured of a fair trial in the courts. Kruger and his Executive Council could bring such pressure to bear upon the Transvaal Supreme Court that it bowed to his dictates. In 1897 the condition became so scandalous that the Boer judges themselves closed the court, declaring it was impossible to administer justice under the coercion to which they were subjected by the executive branch of the government.

This is illustrated by the case of an American named Brown. Brown had staked out mining claims in a district thrown open by the government for pegging. Unfortunately, some of Kruger's official family had been anxious to secure the same claims; hence, they induced Kruger to declare Brown's locations illegal. Brown, of course, appealed to the Supreme Court for validation of his title. When the verdict was handed down in Brown's favor, Kruger dismissed the judges. He then had the Volksraad pass a law that court decisions were subject to revision by the Executive Council of the Transvaal.

Although certain members of the court resigned in protest, it was, nevertheless, a heavy blow to the Uitlanders to find that this last method of securing justice was closed to them because of the influence of Kruger and his entourage.

Among the abuses greatest public prominence was given to the nonpossession of the franchise by the Uitlanders. Although we had founded and built Johannesburg, we had no voice in its civic affairs. The town was created as a mining camp under a mining commissioner. Furthermore, the civil government denied to the Uitlander a free press and right of public meetings. A Boer policeman could at his own discretion disperse any crowd of more than seven.

Prior to 1882, only one year's residence or the possession of land had been required of the immigrant or Uitlander for burgher privileges. At that time the law was amended and five years' residence was requisite, but the entries in the registration books were deliberately falsified by the Boer officials so that few were admitted to the franchise. Then, in 1890, the requirement was increased to fourteen years' residence; furthermore, the Uitlander must be thirty years old, have property, and belong to a Protestant church in order to vote. Every demand made on Kruger to grant the franchise was steadfastly refused.

Pointing to the Vierkleur, he would say, "You see that flag? If I grant the franchise, I may as well pull it down."

The Boers were by no means of one mind as to the justice or the expediency of Kruger's policy regarding the franchise of the Uitlanders. In 1895, thirty-five thousand Uitlanders signed a petition asking for political representation. A prominent member of the Volksraad named Jeppe addressed that body in a speech worthy of Patrick Henry:

This petition has been signed by practically the entire population of the Rand. It contains the name of the millionaire capitalist on the same page as that of the miner; that of the owner of half a district next to that of a clerk. It embraces also all nationalities. And it bears, too, the signatures of some who have been born in this country, who know no other fatherland than this republic, but whom the law regards as strangers. Then, too, there are the newcomers. They have settled for good. They have built Johannesburg, one of the wonders of the age. They own half the soil;

they pay at least three-quarters of the taxes. Nor are they persons who belong to a subservient race. They come from countries where they freely exercise political rights, which can never be long denied to free-born men. Dare we refer them to the present law, which first expects them to wait for fourteen years, and even then pledges itself to nothing? It is a law which denies all rights even to their children born in this country. What will become of us or our children on the day when we shall find ourselves in a minority or perhaps one in twenty, without a single friend among the other nineteen, among those who will then tell us they wished to be brothers, but we by our own act made them strangers in the republic? Old as the world is, has any attempt like ours ever succeeded for long?

*　　　*　　　*

The Reform Movement, as I have explained, had been tardy in inception and was slow to gather momentum. It had begun with conversation, was continued in press discussion, and was protracted by fruitless deputations to Pretoria.

Protests were being made through two bodies. The first was the Transvaal National Union, of which Charles Leonard was chairman. Although more vocal than influential, it had long been carrying on agitation for constitutional rights and had issued much literature in behalf of the unenfranchised.

The second body of protest was the Chamber of Mines, composed of influential businessmen. Although Kruger never granted a charter of incorporation, it met frequently for business reasons and often presented statements of abuses and grievances to the Volksraad.

The Reform Movement as a whole was Fascist rather than Bolshevik in its nature. Direct action was finally undertaken by a group of hard-headed, successful, conservative men of affairs, not by hot-headed, irresponsible radicals. It was the moneyed element in the revolt that finally assumed the leadership. But it was not until the late summer of 1895 that we of the mining interests actively associated ourselves with the movement. Only as a last resort will men representing vested interests risk property and life by entering into a revolution in behalf of good government.

II. CAUSED BY CAPITALIST PROFITEERS?

The charge that the South African War was brought about by the mine owners and their financial allies was expressed by a number of writers, even as early as 1899. The most vigorous and best-supported statement of this case was made by the brilliant British economist and journalist, John A. Hobson (1858–1940). As an employee of the *Manchester Guardian* he travelled through South Africa in the months before the war, interviewing persons in many walks of life. The result was his book, *The War in South Africa, Its Causes and Effects*. He argues forcefully that the much publicized grievances of the Uit-landers were not only exaggerated, but were in fact deliberately fomented by a small group of mining magnates to serve their own ends. He then analyzes the reasons why the "capitalist" interests sought intervention by the British government. Hobson was an acute and original thinker, the author of some 35 books and numerous articles. Perhaps his best known work is *Imperialism: A Study* (1902), a work which exercised a long-standing influence on the interpretation of imperialism.

A Small Confederacy of International Mine-Owners

J. A. HOBSON

THE HELOTS IN JOHANNESBURG

I take it that the motive which has led the majority of English people to approve, so far as they have approved, the policy of their Government, is not their convictions on the merits of the franchise or the suzerainty issues, but a deep and genuine belief that British subjects were grievously oppressed by the Boer Government, and were without security of life, liberty, and property. A recent issue of the *Nineteenth Century* contains a statement from Sir Sidney Sheppard that "neither their persons nor their property can be held safe during the present *régime*." Those who are responsible for working public opinion have been wisely aware that the most effective means of rousing British anger against the Transvaal was to reiterate the statement that English people in Johannesburg were subject to brutal ill-treatment and went about in fear of their lives. I found it very difficult to persuade people upon the spot of the prevalence of this English view of their grievances; and no wonder, for the audacity of the misrepresentation is almost incredible. When I left England, filled with the atrocities of Mr. Chamberlain's Blue-book and Canon Knox Little's commentary upon Boer character, I looked forward to my sojourn in Johannesburg with deep apprehension. I pictured in my mind the oppressed helot of Sir Alfred Milner's famous telegram, continually harried in the peaceful pursuit of his calling by extortionate officials, subject to the personal violence of the brutal "Zarp" in the public streets, and liable to have the privacy of his domestic hearth invaded by blackmailing detectives. The slightest breach of arbitrary and vexatious regulations would, I was assured, be seized upon as a pretext for arrest and fine, while an appeal to the justice of the courts would only add insult to injury. The first doubts of the accuracy of this picture were instilled into my mind on the voyage out in the good ship the *Carisbrook Castle,* by a fellow-passenger who had for some years played an active part in the Outlander movement of Johannesburg. On questioning him respecting the reign of terror on the Rand, he smilingly explained to me that these outrages and sensational grievances were only designed for British consumption; that Britishers got what they wanted and did as they liked in Johannesburg; that the one real grievance which they suffered and resented was the "cocky" and insolent tone of the Boers with whom they came into contact. These people despised the British, and lost no opportunity of showing that they regarded them as inferiors and as cowards. This, in his eyes, was intolerable, and was only to be cured by giving the Boer a downright good thrashing, that he might know his place.

After a month's close inquiry on the spot, I became convinced that this view correctly represented the feeling of the great majority of Outlanders of British birth, or did so before they had been lashed into a brief enthusiasm for franchise and other reforms by a handful of politicians. I am not condemning these demands for reform, many, if not most, of which were both desirable and feasible; but I am convinced that, until the agitation of the last year, the concrete grievances which arouse the sympathy and indignation of the British public lay very

From J. A. Hobson, *The War in South Africa, Its Causes and Effects,* 2nd ed. (London: James Nisbet and Co. Ltd., 1900), pp. 52–61; 229–235; 239–240.

lightly on the soul of the average Outlander. When I began to examine upon the spot, I found plenty of men at the Rand Club and elsewhere who told me startling tales of police brutality and miscarriages of justice, and launched into wholesale denunciations of Boer misgovernment. But two things soon struck me. My informants either confined themselves to generalities unbacked by specific cases, or more commonly narrated wrongs inflicted upon some friend of theirs. When I asked a man to give me instances of injuries or indignities which he himself had experienced, he generally allowed that he had been fortunately immune. Again, I soon observed the same stories coming up with insignificant variations; the story of the detectives who, seeing a man engaged in a harmless game of cards in his own house, forced their way in and hauled him to the charge-house under the Gambling Act; the police who came to the manager of an insurance business, and informed him that a building heavily insured was about to be attacked by incendiaries, and that, unless they were well paid for protecting it, it would certainly be destroyed. I soon became aware that these tales of wrong formed a stage army, the paucity of which was tricked out by continual reiteration. Again, it was nearly always the politician, the member of the League or the Outlander Council, who was so anxious to impress upon me the perils of the streets, the brutality of the "Zarp," the injustice of the courts. As I came more freely into contact with all sorts and conditions of men — the quiet professional man, the shop assistant, the mining overseer — I found these things played no part whatever in his life. Grumblers they were one and all, as healthy Britishers always are; many of them hated the Boer, and believed him corrupt and incompetent; some of them exhibited a certain fervour on the franchise issue; but none of them had undergone any serious personal trouble with police or other officers of State. Several young men told me they had been for years in the habit of knocking about Johannesburg at night

and returning home to the suburbs early in the morning, but that they had never been subjected to any interference. This view was certainly borne out by my personal experience. During the weeks I spent there, public feeling ran high, and then, if at any time, it would seem reasonable to expect scenes of disorder and even riot. But never have I seen a large English town more quiet or more orderly at night than Johannesburg. Though a great deal of drinking goes on at the bars, where the company (Outlanders almost to a man) has often a most disreputable aspect, there was scarcely any of the street-brawling which I saw in Cape Town. Where occasionally a noisy tippler staggered by, the neighbouring "Zarp," with orthodox official delicacy, generally looked the other way, though the delinquent was in most instances one of the Britishers who wanted his country. I have no desire to whitewash Johannesburg or its administration; there is much reason to suppose its police to be more bribable than those of London, and more ignorant and incapable; but I saw literally no indication of the prevailing terrorism and oppression, the insecurity of person and property, charged against it, nor did my cross-examination of many Outlanders elicit any material support for such accusations.

That the machinery for the detection and punishment of crime has reached any high standard of excellence may certainly be doubted. When the rapid growth of this huge cosmopolitan city, with its environment of gold mines, peopled by ten thousand white and nearly a hundred thousand black miners, is taken into consideration, it will be recognised as most unfair to compare the order and government of Johannesburg with those of Manchester or Glasgow. On this matter the testimony of Sir William Butler is more to the point, who compared the condition of the Rand with that of the Californian and Australian goldfields, which he knew well, and who considered the former incomparably superior in all the elements of orderly government. But what about the Edgar case, the Appelbe case, the Cape "boy" cases, and the other villainies? The answer is a simple one. The very hubbub created by these matters, and the monopoly of public interest they aroused, are sufficient to mark their exceptional character. Is there any large town in Europe where one could not cull from the police courts and the nightly streets a crop of similar charges? Assuming all these charges to be true, what did they prove? Nothing, unless they were shown to be indicative of a general condition of misgovernment. No such thing has been shown of Johannesburg. Sir Alfred Milner, prompted by his advisers from the Rand, has literally scooped together every specious example of injustice or tyranny that could be obtained. I make bold to say that he is quite unable to show that these cases are indicative of any general conditions. Indeed, at least one of them may be turned against him. If the Transvaal were really the semi-barbarous country which it is sometimes described as being, is it likely that a policeman shooting a criminal caught red-handed and in violent resistance would be promptly charged with manslaughter and brought to trial? It is very doubtful whether a policeman in one of the Western States of America shooting an Outlander under similar circumstances would even be put upon his trial. In Johannesburg he was charged, tried, and, in the judgment of any one who takes the trouble to read the evidence, fairly acquitted.

*   *   *

But what about the tyrannical laws against the freedom of the press and the right of public meeting, which bulk so big in the parade of grievances? The Outlander politician sometimes sought to persuade me that he had been robbed by law of the very elements of liberty of expression. But on examining these laws, I did not find them differ in form or spirit from the laws which stand upon the statute book of England and other European States.

The Press Law of 1896, against which so loud an outcry was raised when it was used for the temporary suppression of the *Critic* and the *Star,* contains no more oppressive powers than are contained and have been enforced within the last few years in the English law. In Ireland and in India during recent years many prosecutions have been instituted for offences which were venial as compared with those habitually committed by the Johannesburg press. Day after day, in defiance of the Press Law, the *Leader* and the *Star* continued to urge the grossest charges against the President, the Executive, and the Judiciary of the land, and to call on the hostile arms of England to cleanse the Augean stable. One cannot read the language of this press, some examples of which I give in a later chapter, without wondering at the apathy of a Government which could tolerate such abuse.

The Law of Public Meeting is a close copy of the English law in its general regulations regarding the limitations of the right of public meeting. It acknowledges the general right of meeting, but limits that right in the interest of public order, refusing it in cases of meetings "which have for their object disobedience or breach of the law or any legal enactment, disturbance of the rights of any one, the use of forcible means whereby public peace and safety are or may be endangered, or whereby the authority of constituted powers and officials is attacked, or whereby good morals are assailed," &c. It differs from the English law, and is assimilated to the special law for Ireland, in vesting in the police the right to be present at every public meeting, to decide whether it is illegal, and to disperse illegal meetings.

Until last autumn, upon the eve of war, no prosecution under this law had taken place: it was then applied in the case of a disorderly street meeting.

In the Transvaal, as in England, there are laws upon the statute book which, when quoted, sound like terrible restrictions upon liberty, but which as administered, or rather not administered, are harmless. Let me mention one or two crucial facts. Last summer you could stand at any street corner in Johannesburg, within hearing of the "Zarp," and hear Englishmen loudly and bitterly lamenting the sluggishness of the British arms they had invoked to invade the country which had given them shelter and gold; in any bar or other public place you might hear the most vehement denunciations of the Boer Government, and meetings were freely held to advocate the destruction of "the corrupt oligarchy at Pretoria." In front of the stationers' shops of Commissioner Street were displayed the most insulting caricatures of President Kruger, accompanied by letterpress which would not be tolerated by the officials or the public of any European city.

*   *   *

As for general liberty and even license of conduct, it existed nowhere if not in Johannesburg. Every luxury of life, every extravagance of behaviour, every form of private vice flourished unchecked; every man and woman (except Kaffirs, who do the work and don't count) said and did what seemed good in his or her own eyes. The helot wore his golden chains with insolent composure of demeanour, as he feasted in the sumptuous rooms of the Rand and the New Clubs, or lolled in the rickshaw which, drawn by the toiling Kaffir, bore him to his luxurious home. The entire wealth of the country, drawn from the bowels of the earth by Kaffir labour, passed easily into his hands, with the exception of a toll taken by the Government, which he resented as if it were the fruits of the toil of his own hands; in a land of simple-mannered, plain-living farmers he alone had material luxury and the leisure to enjoy it.

*   *   *

FOR WHAT ARE WE FIGHTING?

In former chapters I have shown who the persons are that have brought about

this war and the methods they have employed — a small confederacy of international financiers working through a kept press. It remains to describe the nature and the size of the gain which is their object.

There is no secret about the matter. This war is a terrible disaster for every one else in England and South Africa, but for the mine owners it means a large increase of profits from a more economical working of the mines, and from speculative operations. Mr. Fitzpatrick puts into the mouth of "leading men of the Rand" the following statement of grievances in 1896. "If you want the chief economic grievances they are: The Netherlands Railway Concession, the dynamite monopoly, the liquor traffic, and native labour, which together constitute an unwarrantable burden of indirect taxation on the industry of over two and a half millions sterling annually." In others words, the mining capitalists stood to gain an income of two millions and a half by a successful political or military coup. Mr. Hays Hammond, of the Consolidated Goldfields, "would regard the sum of 6s. per ton as a conservative estimate of the direct and indirect benefits of good government," while Mr. J. B. Robinson takes 6s. as a minimum statement of the gain. Now, Mr. Hammond shows that a saving of 6s. per ton works out at "an increase of annual dividends by £2,413,268, based on last year's tonnage of ore crushed" — an independent corroboration of Mr. Fitzpatrick's former estimate.

Here is something worth spilling the blood of other people for. How is this prize to be won? Mr. Hammond's report contains an ingenuous admission that "in the Transvaal economics and politics are so closely connected," which throws light upon the ways and means of mining economy. Each one of the "savings" he specifies depends upon politics being managed in the interest of the mines. Into the details of these politics I cannot enter. It must suffice to say that dynamite, railway rates, gold thefts, and other matters which figure prominently here and elsewhere are of quite subordinate importance.

The abolition of the dynamite monopoly, for instance, cannot possibly account for more than a quarter of a million increased profits, while a most generous reduction of railway rates, and the best possible administration of the gold theft law would not furnish another tithe of the anticipated gain.

The one all-important object is to secure a full, cheap, regular, submissive supply of Kaffir and white labour. Wages form about 55 per cent. of the working expenses of the mines, and of the 6s. per ton in which Mr. Hammond expresses the advantages of "good government," another expert, Mr. Curle, estimates that 5s. would accrue from a full supply of labour, with proper administration of the Pass and Liquor Laws, which keep the Kaffirs from deserting their employment, and prevent them from obtaining drink.

The attitude of the mining industry towards the Transvaal Government in respect of the labour question is instructive. Witnesses before the Industrial Commission at Johannesburg were unanimous in maintaining that it was the duty of the Government to procure a steady and sufficient supply of Kaffirs for the mines. The Government was called upon to accredit and assist agents of the mining industry to obtain native labour, to "pay premiums to Kaffir chiefs," to furnish extra pay to native Commissioners for the same object, to convey this labour "under supervision" to the mines, erecting "compounds" along the road, reducing railway fares to one-third of the existing rate, and in a dozen other ways spending public money to serve the private interests of the mines. Why "politics and economics are so closely connected" that the public purse should be used to keep down the wages-bill of the mines is not intelligible to English people. But it is perfectly clear that under a "reformed" Government the mine owners will take every care to press these claims.

Put in a concise form, it may be said that this war is being waged in order to secure for the mines a cheap adequate supply of labour. This need has been a pressing and a growing one. The last report of the Chamber of Mines puts the matter thus: "Under the permanent condition of shortage of supply which has prevailed, it is clear that under stress of competition the tendency would have been to gradually increase wages." Last June this "shortage" was estimated at 12,000, in spite of every effort of the Native Labour Association, which scoured Africa to procure Kaffir workers. Sierra Leone, the Gold Coast, and Liberia have been approached by the mine owners, and serious proposals have been entertained to import Hindoo or even Italian labour.

If the output of gold is to be enlarged, on terms which will yield a maximum of profits, a large expansion of the labour-market is essential. It is this issue which beyond all others has driven the capitalists into politics, marking out for them, on the one hand, an imperialist, on the other, a domestic policy. The sources of native labour in the Republics and the Colonies are quite inadequate. The natives of Zululand, Basutoland, Swaziland, and Natal are fine workers, but can seldom be persuaded to go underground, while the Bechuanas and Cape Kaffirs are capricious, and form a very small proportion of the supply. A larger but very unreliable supply comes from the extreme north of the Transvaal: it is significant that no natives from the neighbourhood can be induced to enter the mines. By far the most important supply comes from the Portuguese territories on the east coast, and it is to this quarter and to the lands north of the Zambezi that the mine owners are looking for this increased supply.

It is thus manifest that the pressure of the powerful mining interests will continually be used to drive us into political interference with countries which lie outside our present possession and control. By persuasion or coercion, labour must be got from Mozambique and from the north.

For this reason our international capitalists are expanders of the British Empire.

The difficulty of raising, at a sufficient pace, the required supply from these distant regions will, however, prove very great, and these sources must be supplemented by bringing more pressure to bear upon the reluctant natives of South Africa, among whom underground work is unpopular.

"They should," as Mr. Rudd recently urged, "try some cogent form of inducement or practically compel the native, through taxation or in some other way, to contribute his quota to the good of the community, and to a certain extent he would then have to work." Not only would he have to work, but he would have to work cheap, for, as Mr. Hays Hammond said, "With good government there will be an abundance of labour, and with an abundance of labour there will be no difficulty in cutting down wages."

The thin edge of the wedge of "forced labour" has been introduced in several directions outside of Rhodesia, where, under a thin disguise, it is still in practice; even in Cape Colony Mr. Rhodes, by his Glen Grey Act, has essayed to teach "the dignity of labour" to reluctant natives who prefer to work or idle for themselves, while the forced indenturing of captive Bechuanas charged with, but not convicted of, rebellion, is a line which may be profitably followed in the future, when the present conflict of white races has borne its certain fruit of native disturbances. The Boer treatment of natives in the Transvaal has never been enlightened or humane, and a form of indenture not widely differing from slavery has always prevailed. The fact that some philanthropic persons believe the present war justified by the need of redressing native grievances will not deter our economic lords from adapting the temper and the forms of Boer institutions to their profitable use.

An interesting passage in a recent speech of Earl Grey, referring primarily to Rhodesia, has a likely bearing on the Transvaal mines:

"They must dismiss from their minds the idea of developing their mines with white labour. Means had to be sought to induce the natives to seek, spontaneously, employment at the mines, and to work willingly for long terms of more or less continuous service. In time, he believed, the education of the natives would cause them to seek work to gratify those growing wants which were the certain result of increasing contact with civilisation. Meanwhile, an incentive to labour must be provided by the imposition of a hut-tax of at least £1, in conformity to the practice of Basutoland, and also by the establishment of a small labour-tax, which those able-bodied natives should be required to pay who are unable to show a certificate for four months' work."

There is a humorous impudence in the suggestion that "spontaneous" and "willing" work is to be induced by hut and labour taxes. This is the spirit of South African capitalism all over: the Rand differs from Rhodesia only in being a little less free-spoken — the men are the same, the motives and the economic needs are the same, the conduct will be the same.

There is in reality but one idea of handling the labour problem throughout South Africa, that of "forced labour," thinly disguised under the cloak of taxation, voluntary contract, indenture, or imprisonment. Mr. Rhodes has frequently and openly avowed the economic principle, and has practised it unblushingly in Rhodesia, as the official report of Sir R. Martin testifies.

Mr. Rudd recently maintained with some real show of *à fortiori* reasoning the following interesting thesis:—

"If under the cry of civilisation we in Egypt lately mowed down 10,000 or 20,000 Dervishes with Maxims, surely it cannot be considered a hardship to compel the natives in South Africa to give three months in the year to do a little honest work."

The only obstacle Mr. Rudd sees is the fact that "there is a morbid sentimentality among a large section of the community on the question of the natives"; in other words, the moral feelings which according to Mr. Hugh Price Hughes and his friends are the chief justification of this war. In his examination before the Industrial Commission Mr. Albu gave the following interesting evidence upon the wage question:

"The native at the present time receives a wage which is far in excess of the exigencies of his existence. The native earns between 50s. and 60s. per month, and then he pays nothing for food or lodging, in fact he can save almost the whole amount he receives. . . . If the native can save £20 a year, it is almost sufficient for him to go home and live on the fat of his land. In five or six years' time the native population will have saved enough money to make it unnecessary for them to work any more. The consequences of this will be most disastrous for the industry and the State. This question applies to any class of labour, and in any country, whether it be in Africa, Europe, or America. I think if the native gets enough pay to save £5 a year, that sum is quite enough for his requirements, and will prevent natives from becoming rich in a short space of time."

*   *   *

Though less has been said, for obvious reasons, about reducing white wages, miners are well aware of the intention of the managers, and Mr. Albu's sentiments are known to be widely entertained. The matter is well put in a recent article by "An Outlander" published in the *Mining World*:—

"White wages have not been reduced in the past, because the Outlanders desired to work together for political salvation, and any attack upon the white labourers' pay would have caused a split in the ranks. However, when new conditions prevail, white wages must come down."

Indeed, the saving to be effected out of white wages is greater than out of black, for the aggregate of the wages paid to white miners has hitherto been larger than that paid to black, though the numbers of the latter are eight times as large.

If this war can be successfully accomplished, and a "settlement" satisfactory to the mine owners can be reached, the first fruits of victory will be represented in a large, cheap, submissive supply of black and white labour, attended by such other economies of "costs" as will add millions per annum to the profits of the mines. It is no extravagance to argue that the blood and the money of the people of Great Britain are being spent for this purpose; that at present no other definite tangible result of the conflict can be shown. The men who, owning the South African press and political organisations, engineered the agitation which has issued in this war, are the same men whose pockets will swell with this increase; open-eyed and persistent they have pursued their course, plunging South Africa into a temporary ruin in order that they may emerge victorious, a small confederacy of international mine-owners and speculators holding the treasures of South Africa in the hollow of their hands.

III. CAUSED BY JAMESON'S "CRIMINAL BLUNDER"?

Partly because of its dramatic qualities, the Jameson Raid has always been assigned a prominent place as a cause of the Anglo-Boer War. Assessment of the episode has been complicated by the question as to whether British officials, chiefly the Colonial Secretary, were directly involved in the conspiracy which led to the Raid. The first reading in this section is by the English historian, R. C. K. Ensor, whose volume, *England 1870–1914*, has been for many years one of the best scholarly treatments of the period. Mr. Ensor (1877–1958) had a varied career as a lawyer, a journalist, a public servant, and ultimately a research fellow at Oxford University. Although he agrees with other writers as to the baneful effects of the Raid, Ensor accepts the view that Chamberlain knew nothing about Rhodes' plan to invade the Transvaal.

The second reading, by Miss Ethel Drus, takes direct issue with Ensor on the point of official government complicity. Miss Drus had her early training at Cape Town and is now Lecturer in History at the University of Hull. In addition to the article which is in part reproduced here, the author has also edited papers of Joseph Chamberlain relating to the Raid, and, in another article, papers relating to Anglo-Transvaal relations, 1896–1899. In the latter portion of the article, not printed here, Miss Drus raises questions as to the involvement of the Cabinet, and even of members of the former Liberal government.

The third reading is by the South African historian, Dr. Jean van der Poel, whose book, *The Jameson Raid*, was the first full-length study to make use of new materials which had become available to scholars in the South African archives. Dr. van der Poel is Senior Lecturer in History at the University of Cape Town. The selection presents her conclusions as to the effects of the Raid.

Chamberlain Did Not Foreknow the Raid

R. C. K. ENSOR

THE most anxious problem before the new colonial secretary lay in South Africa, where affairs in the Transvaal were working up to a crisis. We saw above how that republic was left after the London Convention of 1884. In 1886 occurred a development which Wolseley had forecast as likely, but the British government had left out of account. A goldfield of extraordinary richness was discovered on the Witwatersrand. Foreigners, mostly (but by no means all) British subjects, flocked in to exploit it; and year after year, as the mines developed, their population grew. Johannesburg became a great city. The attitude of the Transvaal government under Kruger towards the new-comers — "Uitlanders" as they were called — was from the first uncompromising. "We will not exclude you," they said in effect, "but this is our country, and if you come here to seek wealth, it must be entirely on our terms. They are that you shall have no votes and no rights, and we shall so tax you, both directly on the mine profits and indirectly by enormous duties on imported mine-requisites, that a large part of what you get will pass to us." The Uitlanders preferred coming even on this footing to not coming at all; and Kruger treated their doing so as justifying any hardship that he might care to put on them. "They need not have come," was his refrain, "but having come they must abide the consequences." "You need not have admitted them," was the British retort later on, "but having admitted them, you must treat them justly."

The upshot was that the treasury of the Transvaal, which had been the poorest, soon became the richest in South Africa.

Kruger's ambitions rose. He bought extensive armaments. He had glimpses of a Boer paramountcy. From Europe he engaged clever Dutch civil servants; and these "Hollanders," as they were called, naturally strengthened the anti-English bias to which they owed their posts. They helped him to coquet with European Powers, particularly Germany. Here there was an obstacle in the 1884 Convention, which debarred the Transvaal from treating with foreign governments, other than that of the Orange Free State, except through Great Britain. Nothwithstanding it, he made contacts with Berlin; and on 27 January 1895, addressing a *Kaiser-Kommers* [a convivial meeting to celebrate the German emperor's birthday] held by German residents in the Transvaal, he publicly indicated their purpose.

Two earlier episodes had some bearing on his attitude. The first went back to November 1884, when a British force of 4,000 men under Sir Charles Warren put an end to obstinate Boer encroachments in Bechuanaland and compelled respect for the frontier fixed nine months earlier by the London Convention. This hemmed the Transvaal on the west; while later the Chartered Company's acquisition of Rhodesia hemmed it on the north. The second episode was a treaty regarding Swaziland and Tongaland made by Lord Ripon with the Transvaal in December 1894. Under it, after years of dispute, Kruger obtained Swaziland as a protectorate; but Tongaland, the coastal strip between it and sea, was earmarked by Great Britain. He had been much set on getting a port of his own, and this final exclusion from salt water mortified and rankled with him intensely.

From R. C. K. Ensor, *England 1870–1914*, Vol. XIV of *The Oxford History of England*, ed. G. N. Clark (Oxford, 1936), pp. 226–236. Reprinted by permission of The Clarendon Press, Oxford.

Over against Kruger in South Africa stood as his main adversary Cecil Rhodes. Then the "Colossus" of politics and finance, he led not merely the British but the Cape Dutch; whose party, the "Bond," made him premier at Capetown, and who resented Kruger's hostility to the Cape's trade. Rhodes, besides being managing director of the Chartered Company, had large interests on the Rand; and his brother Frank was a leader of the Johannesburg Uitlanders. At Westminster he had friends in all camps, but his favourite on the front benches was Lord Rosebery; and he seems to have preferred his government to any other. Under it he had been negotiating with the colonial office for Bechuanaland. His company coveted all that it could get. But its minimum need was a strip along the Transvaal frontier, in order to carry the Capetown-Kimberley railway up to Rhodesia. It already ran north as far as Mafeking, and the area up to that point — known as "British" Bechuanaland — had been promised to the Cape government, of which he was head.

So Chamberlain's initial autumn in office confronted him with three problems — first, Rhodes's claims to Bechuanaland; secondly, a dispute with Kruger over trade across the Vaal; thirdly, an agitation, growing for some time past, among the Rand Uitlanders. As to the first, he carried out the promise that the Cape should have "British" Bechuanaland; but of the Bechuanaland Protectorate beyond it, which Rhodes claimed for the Chartered Company, he refused to concede more than the narrow strip for the projected railway. This was because three Bechuana chiefs, of whom Khama was the leader, came to England, and petitioned against being placed under chartered rule. In the conceded strip, however, the company was granted policing rights, as elsewhere in its territories. The dispute with Kruger arose from the desire of the latter to discourage imports through the Cape in favour of imports through non-British Delagoa Bay — the Portuguese harbour whose railway to

Pretoria was opened on 8 July of that year. He first held up traffic on the railway from the Vaal to the Rand, and then, when an ox-wagon service was organized instead from the south bank, closed the "drifts" (i.e. fords) on the river. These were breaches of Article XIII of the 1884 Convention; and Chamberlain, having Cape opinion behind him, dispatched on 3 November 1895 a veiled but unmistakable ultimatum. Kruger gave way.

Meanwhile the Uitlanders in Johannesburg were almost ostentatiously conspiring to rebel. A petition signed by over 35,000 of them in August had been rejected. Their wrongs and claims had for a year been occupying Chamberlain's predecessor, Lord Ripon; who that summer in sending out a new high commissioner, Sir Hercules Robinson, had said that "what he most feared, was a rising at Johannesburg." Chamberlain, therefore, fully expected one, and after consulting Lord Salisbury had approved a plan to meet it; which was that on its outbreak the high commissioner as representative of the paramount Power should travel to Pretoria, and mediate between Kruger and the rebels.

Rhodes, however, unknown to either Chamberlain or Robinson, had quite a different scheme. It was to assemble as large a force of mounted police as the Chartered Company could muster at a "jumping-off ground" on the newly acquired strip. Dr. Jameson, the company's administrator, was to command them, and on a signal they were to make an armed dash for Johannesburg. This, of course, meant pure filibustering; and as against a state, like the Transvaal, with which we were at peace, it was utterly indefensible.

At the brink of crisis an event occurred which warped the whole British situation. On 17 December 1895 Grover Cleveland, president of the United States, sent a message to Congress. It was virtually an ultimatum to Great Britain. The subject was the boundary between British Guiana and Venezuela, about which negotiations had long been in progress between London and

Caracas. Venezuela was claiming on historical grounds a large part of British Guiana, and had thoughtfully given a concession there to an American syndicate. Cleveland was within a year of the time when he must stand, if at all, for re-election. He was a gold democrat, and the tide of bimetallism, which was to sweep his party in 1896, already wetted his feet. "Twisting the lion's tail" was still a strong card to play in American politics. In his message he announced that he would appoint an American commission to define the boundary, and impose its award upon Great Britain — by war, if necessary — in the name of the Monroe Doctrine.

This was certainly one of the most unexpected, least warranted, and least excusable steps ever taken in modern times by a Great Power. Its direct consequences need not detain us long. The message evoked a frenzy of Jingoism throughout the United States; but a chastening influence was exerted by a catastrophic fall in American stocks. British opinion displayed restraint from the start. It became obvious that, while an Anglo-American war would still be the most popular of all wars in America, in England it was viewed as fratricidal. Cleveland appointed his Commission; but it was composed of prudent men, and Lord Salisbury accepted its invitation to supply it with documents of the British case. Meanwhile Chamberlain, who had an American wife, was active behind the scenes; first using as intermediary the veteran Lord Playfair (also married to an American), and later, in September 1896, visiting the United States and interviewing Cleveland's secretary of state, Olney, in private. The result of these talks was the Treaty of Washington (2 February 1897), by which the question was referred to arbitration. The award (promulgated on 3 October 1899) confirmed all the principal British claims.

But the indirect consequences went much farther. The Cleveland message laid bare the isolation of Great Britain. Had war resulted, it might have been 1779 over

again, with Germany heading a hostile Europe against us. Already in October there had been a wrangle between London and Berlin over Germany's support of Kruger. The message was perhaps decisive in confirming the Wilhelmstrasse's anti-British orientation. It may, too, have helped to precipitate Rhodes's action, for since Kruger's *Kaiser-Kommers* speech the German peril weighed especially with him. But it also helped to divide and unman the Rand plotters; since among them were not a few Americans and Germans, and a doubt was opened up if Great Britain's could be the winning side. At the last moment they were paralysed by a dispute whether in revolting they should hoist the British or the Transvaal flag. On 27 December Robinson cabled to Chamberlain that the movement had collapsed. Next day Rhodes at the Cape said the same to Sir Graham Bower, the imperial secretary. All this time Dr. Jameson had been waiting in the corridor north of Mafeking in pursuance of Rhodes's design. From Johannesburg and even from Rhodes's factotum, Dr. Rutherfoord Harris, he received discouraging messages. But none came from Rhodes himself; and on the evening of 29 December the "Raid" was launched.

Jameson had 350 Chartered police with him at Pitsani, and 120 Bechuanaland police placed under his orders joined him on the road. With this body of 470 mounted men, 8 machine-guns, and 3 pieces of artillery, he planned to reach Johannesburg, 180 miles distant, before the Boers could stop him. Apart from the criminality of the enterprise, it was an absurd miscalculation of force, only to be explained by the Chartered men's misvaluing of their Matabele victories. "If Isandhlwana could be wiped out by machine-guns," they seem to have reasoned, "why not Majuba too?" Events soon undeceived them. Near Krugersdorp on their fourth day out the raiders were halted by deadly fire from invisible Boers. Next morning (2 January 1896) they were manœuvered at Doornkop into a complete trap; and on a promise that their lives would be spared, laid down their arms. Their captor was Commandant Cronje. They had about forty casualties, including sixteen killed; the Boer casualties were under ten.

Till 29 December Chamberlain had had no inkling that anything like the Raid would happen. Receiving then a vague report that it might, he cabled strongly to Robinson against it—repeating his monition in the most emphatic terms when news of the start reached him thirty-six hours later. Following the first cable Robinson had a courier sent after Jameson; who overtook him when two days out, and ordered him in the queen's name to desist, but he refused. Following the second, he issued a drastic proclamation against the raiders. Meanwhile Chamberlain himself sternly denounced them to the Chartered Company, and telegraphed a direct repudiation to President Kruger. These steps he took while the result was still in the balance, and in defiance of the company's attempt (by publishing a faked letter alleging that women and children had been in danger at Johannesburg) to make the raiders popular heroes. Stronger prima facie proof, that he neither foreknew nor favoured nor condoned that particular crime, he could scarcely have given.

Rhodes's guilt was obvious, and he resigned the Cape premiership. But the day after Jameson's surrender produced a new complication — the celebrated "Kruger telegram." The German emperor cabled to the Transvaal president (3 January 1896): "I sincerely congratulate you that, without appealing for the help of friendly Powers, you with your people, by your own energy against the armed hordes which as disturbers of the peace broke into your country, have succeeded in re-establishing peace and maintaining the independence of your country against attacks from without." Though sometimes afterwards ascribed to a random impulse of the Kaiser, this message, implying Germany's right and intention to interfere in the Transvaal contrary to the 1884 Convention, was in fact a most

deliberate act of state. It is now known that it emanated from a conference held by William II, at which the chancellor, foreign minister, and three others were present. Nor did it stand alone; orders were sent to ship colonial troops from German East Africa to Delagoa Bay, whence with a naval detachment from three German cruisers already lying off Lourenço Marques they were to go by rail to Pretoria. Had they done so, war could scarcely have been avoided; but the Portuguese stood firm and refused transit.

Down to this telegram the wider English public, nettled by fourteen years of persistent French opposition in every quarter of the globe, had assumed that Germany under Queen Victoria's grandson was Great Britain's friend. The disillusionment was keen, and an explosion of anger shook the nation. The government promptly manned and sent to sea a "flying squadron" capable of crushing any other navy afloat, as navies then were. German statesmen felt they had gone too far. They veered to an apologetic tone. But the anti-English policy, whose theorist was Holstein, was not abandoned; and at home from the emperor down they used the "flying squadron" as a new and potent argument for creating a great German navy.

The telegram worsened the South African sequel of the Raid. It blunted British repudiation of Rhodes and the Raiders. Following the fiasco Sir Hercules Robinson hastened to Pretoria — in no position now to mediate with a high hand. Kruger used him to obtain the unconditional surrender of the Johannesburg rebels. Their leaders were put on trial in the Transvaal; four (including Rhodes's brother) were condemned to death, and fifty-nine to various periods of imprisonment with fines of £2,000 each. Chamberlain with difficulty got the death sentences commuted, and the others partially revised. Meanwhile the Raiders had been handed over to the British government; and Jameson with the officers of his force stood in the dock at Bow Street. Sent for trial "at Bar" before three eminent judges, they were convicted and properly sentenced. But the effect on opinion abroad, and especially in the Transvaal, was more than cancelled by a fever of London enthusiasm for the accused. Although in the main a reaction against the Kruger telegram (and chiefly metropolitan at that), it helped foreigners to view the whole nation as Jameson's accomplices. Already on 4 March a pro-Kruger candidate, Marthinus Steyn, had been elected president of the Orange Free State against J. G. Fraser, the leader of the moderate party. A year later (17 March 1897) Steyn signed at Bloemfontein a treaty of offensive and defensive alliance with the Transvaal.

The deeper problems of the Raid's authorship were referred to a select committee of the house of commons. Chamberlain himself was a member, and the opposition representatives included Harcourt, Campbell-Bannerman, and Labouchere. The committee sat five months; heard Chamberlain, Rhodes, and a multitude of witnesses; and reported in July 1897, severely censuring Rhodes, but entirely acquitting Chamberlain and the colonial office. This finding was supported by Harcourt and Campbell-Bannerman, and indeed by the whole committee save Labouchere and an Irish member. But there was a fatal flaw in it. The company's agents, in their anxiety to shelve inquiry, had put about that certain telegrams, sent from London to Capetown before the Raid, contained evidence that Chamberlain had been involved. Before the committee 44 telegrams were produced out of a series of 51, but 7, which it was implied were the incriminating ones, were by Rhodes's order expressly withheld. The committee failed to compel their production, and thereby rendered possible the charge that its members hid the truth to shield Chamberlain. To most Englishmen it was a sufficient answer that men like Harcourt and Campbell-Bannerman were assenting members of the committee. But to foreigners this only made the affair more sinister. Both front benches, thought the

Boers of the Transvaal, were in league against their liberties. The impression was deepened by the ensuing commons debate, when, after Harcourt had spoken powerfully for the colonial secretary, that statesman rose at the end, and while defending the government's decision not to follow up censuring Rhodes by punishing him, slipped in the grievous overstatement that the Colossus had done nothing affecting his "personal position as a man of honour."

What was the truth here? A primary duty of the select committee had been to clear up to the satisfaction of reasonable men, whether at home or abroad, the responsibilities of the British government. Why, by acquiescing in the mystery of the telegrams, did it fail to do so? Again, when Chamberlain signed the committee's report, he subscribed to a most proper censure of Rhodes. Why did he virtually unsay it in his house of commons speech? Sinister explanations were current among well-informed people at the time. It was said that the committee had been influenced by some secret communication from a very high quarter. It was said that Chamberlain made his whitewashing speech under duress, and that a liberal member of parliament sat in the house of commons with the telegrams in his pocket, ready to read them if he did not toe the line. The first story may now, in all its forms, be dismissed, in face of the very categorical denials by Lewis Harcourt, who in 1897 had acted as his father's secretary and knew everything that he knew. But the second may still be true. Harcourt himself regarded Chamberlain's speech as having done nearly all the mischief. He thought also that Chamberlain, while he had a clean sheet in regard to the Raid, had not one in regard to the preparation for a rising in Johannesburg, and that this privity rendered him liable "to something in the nature of 'severe pressure'" by Rhodes and his friends.

Was this so? "My case is," wrote Chamberlain to the permanent head of his Department, "that while I knew all about the revolution, I knew nothing of anything so mad as Jameson's raid." What did his "knowing all about the revolution" cover? The full text of the missing telegrams remains unpublished, but the quasi-incriminating passages in them can now be read. None suffices to rebut the otherwise overwhelming evidence that he did not foreknow the Raid. But more than one would have made an ugly impression if printed at the time; and it seems scarcely doubtful that Dr. Rutherfoord Harris, who was their chief author, had deliberately worded them (and some of their fellows in the Blue Book) with an eye to subsequent blackmail. For sanctioning the vile use made of them the blame is Rhodes's; but why did Chamberlain sit down under it? There are other documents printed by his biographer which may suggest that he feared the alternative. Thus on 18 December 1895, after the Cleveland message, he had written to the head of his department to discuss whether, and in what way, that complication might affect the timing of the Johannesburg revolt. His conclusion was that "either it should come *at once* or be postponed for a year or two at least"; and he asked that a certain high official of the colonial office should communicate this to Rhodes's agent in London, Maguire. This was done; Maguire cabled to Rhodes, with whom were Beit and Harris; and Beit at once wired to Johannesburg "urging instant flotation new Company." Chamberlain himself more than a year later made the marginal comment: "I have no doubt that Beit and Harris were influenced by Maguire's telegram." In short, Downing Street had done something very like pulling the trigger; though without really knowing what trigger it pulled.

Chamberlain might have done better to defy Rhodes and let the facts come out. They were after all less heinous than might at first appear. The Transvaal's was not a friendly government; short of being actually at war it could scarcely have been more hostile. The British Uitlanders, whom Kruger oppressed, formed half of the country's white male population; and a British minister could not be expected to lack sympathy for them. Nor did the rebels really contemplate killing Boers, or "levying war" save in a technical sense; their idea was merely for a dramatic move to enable the high commissioner to intervene. But the result of leaving undetermined the degree of Downing Street's complicity with Rhodes was to cause Dutch South Africa to surmise much worse guilt. It believed Great Britain to have backed the Raid; and the belief was a main stage on the path to eventual war. The Transvaal Boers, who before had been pretty equally divided between Krugerism and progress, were now united by their fears and suspicions. In 1893 Kruger had been re-elected president by 7,854 votes against 7,009 cast for his progressive opponent. In February 1898 he polled 12,858 votes, and his two progressive opponents could not muster 6,000 between them. Nor was the mischief confined to his republic. Before the Raid Rhodes had enjoyed the support of the Dutch in Cape Colony and the trust of those in the Orange Free State. Owing to the Raid he forfeited both. Owing to the proceedings of the select committee and Chamberlain's unhappy speech Great Britain forfeited them likewise. The cause of unity and reconciliation between the two white races in South Africa received an incalculable setback.

British Officials Were Guilty

ETHEL DRUS

In Dr. Jean van der Poel's powerful study of the conspiracy to overthrow the Boer government of the Transvaal Republic at the close of 1895, interest inevitably centres on the indictment of Joseph Chamberlain, the colonial secretary. It is a notorious fact that the committee of inquiry in 1897 acquiesced, for patriotic reasons, in the suppression of vital evidence and hence, as E. T. Cook, of the *Daily News* pointed out, the inquiry "stopped short precisely at the point where it ought to have gone on." In February 1900, after the publication of some stolen documents in *l'Indépendence Belge,* the Radicals in the Commons demanded a fresh inquiry and the production of all relevant papers. The motion was, however, defeated by 286 to 152 votes and thus no new material of importance could be obtained until the publication in 1934 of Garvin's third volume of the biography of Chamberlain. While stoutly asserting that Chamberlain had not "a shadow of complicity with the Raid," he nevertheless printed material of so revealing a character that the old suspicion was merely rekindled and led Professor H. R. Winkler to point to the need for "a re-evaluation of the numerous documents printed in Garvin's work." This became possible when on 1 January 1946 the Bower papers in the South African Public Library at Cape Town were unsealed. Collating these with all the relevant published material, Dr. Jean van der Poel was able to build up a formidable case against Chamberlain. I myself, after an examination of the recently opened files in the Public Record Office in London, and a close scrutiny of the Chamberlain papers, still in private possession, consider that her thesis of complicity would have been strengthened, certainly not weakened, by reference to these sources. In discussing the main points made by Dr. van der Poel, it will be necessary to refer to this supporting evidence. Some of it is contained in my "Report on the Private Papers of Joseph Chamberlain relating to the Jameson Raid and the Inquiry," but where new material has not yet been published, a detailed reference will be given.

What is the charge against Chamberlain? Briefly, that he was fully informed of the so-called Rhodes or Jameson plan to invade the Transvaal and overthrow its government on the pretext of going to the relief of the Uitlanders, and that he abetted it by ceding the Bechuanaland Protectorate with its strategic border strip, and by sanctioning the concentration of an armed force at Pitsani, completely independent of Crown control. Chamberlain's defence, though he shifted his ground from time to time, was that as he had refused to listen to confidences volunteered by Rhodes's agents and had never understood their "guarded allusions," the compromising references to him in "the missing telegrams" (i.e. those withheld from the committee at his command) were due to a distortion of "casual expressions and incidental remarks." Curiously enough, in the same breath, he complained "of the breach of confidence which they (the cables) disclose." This summary of his case is derived from his unpublished memorandum of June 1896 and a private letter to Earl Grey of 13 October 1896. It must, however, be appreciated that he was very much more reticent before the committee of inquiry.

It is not difficult to dispose of the plea

From Ethel Drus, "The Question of Imperial Complicity in the Jameson Raid," *English Historical Review,* LXVIII (1953), pp. 582–587. Reprinted by permission of Ethel Drus, *The English Historical Review,* and Longmans, Green & Co., Ltd.

of ignorance, which depended on his assertion that he had refused to listen to Rhodes's agents. Although it is true that he stopped Dr. Harris at the first interview at the Colonial Office on 1 August 1895, there remained the awkward fact that immediately thereafter he had granted a private interview to Earl Grey, who, as a director of the British South Africa Company, had introduced Harris. When Chamberlain later appealed privately to Grey for support, the latter replied that it was only *after* he had explained Rhodes's design that Chamberlain "declined to receive this information which you said you would be obliged to use officially if it were pressed upon you." Moreover, Chamberlain himself admitted in his memorandum that apparent or official ignorance was essential if he were not to quash the conspiracy. His duty in this respect was very plain. At Jameson's trial the Lord Chief Justice held that no altruistic motive could justify the incursion. ". . . it is one primary duty of the State to seek to respect the independent sovereignty and the inviolability of the territory of the other. If either is attacked it means war." Anyone abetting the offence was himself "a principal offender." Hence it is not unlikely that Chamberlain's dangerous admission was one of the reasons why Lord Salisbury refused to sanction the publication of the memorandum. Nor is it surprising that Grey was not summoned to give evidence at the inquiry and that Chamberlain omitted to inform the committee of their interview.

This foreknowledge alone explains, as Grey observed in the letter cited above, Chamberlain's "subsequent acts." It would appear from the second half of the cable of 2 August 1895, sent shortly after the interview with Grey, that Chamberlain, though refusing an immediate transfer of the whole Protectorate, had offered a "large land grant" as "alternative to justify residence B.S.A. Co. in Protectorate." Its suppression by Garvin, on the scarcely credible pretext that it was in code jargon and quite irrelevant, suggests that he appreciated its

significance. Again, as Dr. van der Poel shows, Chamberlain's urgency in securing for the company the region that became the border base is remarkable. Thus, on 20 August, after the second interview with Harris at the Colonial Office Chamberlain instructed the High Commissioner by cable to secure a grant of land from Chief Bathoen, whose country included Gaberones, then designated as the military base. Yet he knew that the Bechuana chiefs were sailing on the very next day for England to plead passionately against any cession to the company. Nor is it less remarkable that negotiations with two minor chiefs, of uncertain authority, were authorized when Bathoen refused to make any grant. In this manner the Pitsani base was obtained. What is more, it was speedily transferred to the company on 18 October, despite the fact that the obduracy of the leading chiefs prevented a general settlement of the Protectorate until 6 November.

The presence of the armed force at Pitsani also required explanation. Chamberlain could not deny that he had sanctioned, indeed facilitated, recruitment, but he pleaded that he had not had reason to doubt the company's excuse that it was necessary to protect the railway works (not yet begun) from native attacks. Here one finds Chamberlain constantly shifting his ground. In the Commons, on 13 February 1896, he justified the use of the force as a fire brigade benevolently intended to extinguish a blaze in a neighbour's house, though asserting at the same time that to have warned the republic of its danger "would have been rather presumptuous" and unwarranted intervention in its internal affairs. Later, in his memorandum of June 1896, his plea was that the force was only to be used with the sanction of the High Commissioner "under circumstances of immediate danger to life." However, warned by an official of the contradictory arguments he was employing on this head, he assured the committee of inquiry that he had never suspected the true reason. Here he is exposed by the most interesting single document on the Raid remaining in the Colonial Office files — the most important papers were removed by Chamberlain and are now with his private correspondence. When the company's application was received on 21 August 1895, the assistant under-secretary, Fairfield, and Graham, the acting principal clerk, ridiculed the company's allegations of native hostility, declaring them to be wild exaggerations. Graham wrote:

There is no need, nor would it be desirable, to accept the offer of the Co's police. We have still 350 B.B.P. and if they are not enough to keep order it will not be a question of Police at all. I do not see how it is possible for the Company to commence operations before the Octr. rains.

After Graham had searched the files in vain for any record of native disturbances, as instanced by the company, Fairfield prepared a draft querying the company's assertions, and stating that the colonial secretary was averse to the surrender of exclusive Crown control over the armed force. Moreover, as Lord Selborne, the parliamentary under-secretary, objected that obstacles were being raised in the way of railway construction, Fairfield asked Chamberlain to decide, observing, "The principle [sic] question is whether you will make any demur to letting the Company's police come in."

Finally, there is the incontestable fact of Chamberlain's decision against the postponement of the revolt, which, besides making him responsible with Rhodes and Jameson for the later "fiasco," indicates his influential position in the conspiracy. In a letter of 18 December 1895 Sir Robert Meade, the permanent under-secretary, had written to Chamberlain that he and Fairfield, the specialist on South Africa, considered it advisable to stop the movement on account of the quarrel with the United States over the boundary between British Guiana and Venezuela. Chamberlain replied, however, that Fairfield should see Rochfort Maguire, another of Rhodes's

agents, and explain to him that immediate action was preferable to an outbreak coinciding with the crisis in Anglo-American relations. The consequence of that interview was the notorious "hurry up" telegram of 20 December 1895, which arrived at the time when Rhodes was considering the abandonment of the plot, emissaries from Johannesburg having warned him that there was no enthusiasm for rebellion. This cable, and those to the same effect from *The Times,* led him to disregard the warnings he received. Thus, when Bower urged him to go no further, Rhodes retorted that Bower was opposing Chamberlain's own policy. "Then you are disloyal to your chief Chamberlain who is hurrying me up." Chamberlain devoted a considerable amount of space in his memorandom to a justification of his action. He maintained that it had been his duty to intervene as Britain was the paramount power in South Africa, but he also denied that his action had constituted intervention. Again one notes another instance of his inability to perceive the inherent contradiction in his statements. Garvin, however, attempted a rather different defence for Chamberlain on this head, not without its own absurdity. For while on page 73 he suggested that Fairfield, being both frivolous and deaf, had caused "an incidental misunderstanding" resulting in the unfortunate cable of 20 December, on page 112 he flatly denied its existence, stating that the telegram of 7 November was "the seventh and *last* of the missing telegrams." This despite the fact that his source was unquestionably Chamberlain's own memorandum!

To make Chamberlain's innocence more plausible, it was desirable to show that the High Commissioner had been kept in the dark by his own subordinates in South Africa, in particular Sir Graham Bower, the imperial secretary, and F. J. Newton, the resident commissioner of the Bechuanaland Protectorate. Robinson's part was a sorry one. Though he disliked the plot, which he characterized as "a damned conspiracy of Rhodes and Chamberlain," he offered no formal protest, carried out his instructions and thought to ease his conscience and ensure his peerage by professing ignorance. In recent years there has been striking corroboration of Bower's assertion that Robinson was an accessory, albeit an unwilling one. In the *National Review* of December 1934, Viscountess Milner related that when she was in South Africa in 1900 as the wife of Salisbury's son, Lord Edward Cecil, Jameson assured her of Robinson's foreknowledge. Indeed, she had reported this conversation to Chamberlain who agreed that it was "substantially correct." Obviously Lady Milner was unaware of the implications of the High Commissioner's connivance, but it is strange that Chamberlain should have been so incautious.

Raking Up the Raid

JEAN van der POEL

PUBLICATION of concealed evidence could, however, only confirm what the available evidence has already put beyond doubt — that the Colonial Secretary and the High Commissioner were deeply implicated in the conspiracy that caused the Raid. The extent of their complicity may again be shortly stated. They did not, of course, know that Jameson would, in order to force Johannesburg into action, make a dash for the Rand without waiting for a rising. No one knew that but Jameson himself, and even he finally made up his mind to go into the Transvaal only twelve hours before he crossed the border. But the British authorities did join in the conspiracy to bring about a *coup d'état*. This was to begin with a token rising, to be supported by the Chartered troops and to be clinched by the intervention of the High Commissioner who would at once apply a prearranged "settlement." By these means the Colonial Secretary intended to make the Transvaal a British Colony. It was he who made the whole plan possible by transferring the border zone and the police to the Company, knowing the purpose for which they were required. All this was culpable; but still more so was Chamberlain's direction, when the unready plotters hesitated, that they should act at once, do the deed without delay, hurry up and pull the trigger while Great Britain could still intervene effectively.

To absolve the Imperial authorities from blame by separating the preparations for the *coup d'état* from Jameson's bolt and arguing that, although they knew something about the first, they knew nothing about the second, is to resort to the device of the red herring. This was first trailed before the House of Commons by Chamberlain himself in 1896, then it was used before the Committee of Enquiry; forty years later Chamberlain's biographer had recourse to it. Garvin did admit that Chamberlain possessed a far more intimate knowledge of the "preparations" than the Colonial Secretary himself ever publicly owned. But it cannot be gathered from his book what the full extent of Chamberlain's complicity was. His ignorance of Jameson's decision to bolt is irrelevant. His fault consisted in aiding and abetting the Prime Minister of the Cape Colony to overthrow the Government of a neighbour state in order to bring it into a British federation and in spurring on the reluctant conspirators. But for that spurring on at a critical moment Rhodes might have listened sooner to those who were urging him to drop his plan and Jameson might have been deterred in good time from his venture. It was an indefensible act and Chamberlain was determined that it should not be brought home to him. The documents dealing with it remained among the missing evidence. In the Committee of Enquiry the "hurrying up" was not hinted at. Garvin glosses it over and lays it at the door of Maguire and Fairfield on whom, if Bower's statement is true, Chamberlain also had proposed to put the responsibility for it should the evidence come out.

Those who try to separate consent to the Raid from support of the conspiracy that led to it imply that, while the first was culpable, the second was justifiable. But an invasion by Jameson's force was always part of the conspiracy and even if he had waited for the word from Johannesburg, and the *coup d'état* had gone according to

Reprinted by permission of Oxford University Press, Cape Town, from Jean van der Poel, *The Jameson Raid* (Cape Town, 1951), pp. 259–262.

plan, it would still have been a plot against the independence of the Transvaal. It would in that event have been possible to argue that it was a *bona fide* intervention in a spontaneous rising for the purpose of restoring order and preventing bloodshed. But such a representation of the *coup,* even if the world had believed it, would have been a deception, and its perpetration no more justifiable than Jameson's unauthorized raid.

Some of the conspirators pleaded justification of the means by the end. "If we had succeeded," said Jameson, "we would have been forgiven." "What does it matter to me?" said Rhodes, speaking of his summons before the Committee of Enquiry, "I know that I have done what was right." But the Machiavellian plea cannot be maintained, for the end that the imperialists thought they foresaw was in reality unpredictable. Their expectation that the *coup* would at once succeed, that the simultaneous intervention of the Chartered police and the High Commissioner would paralyse the Transvaal Government, that there would be no resistance and a painless transference of control to Great Britain followed by a peaceful federation — all this was an assumption. In reality they were running the risk of throwing South Africa and Great Britain into war.

Had Rhodes and Chamberlain been better statesmen they would have seen the risk and refused to take it, and they would have repudiated the deception inherent in their plan. They would have been content to let the federation of South Africa come about by natural means and at an unforced pace. Powerful cohesive forces were already drawing the two republics and the two colonies together. Their commercial interdependence, their customs and railway linkage, the racial and social affinities of their white inhabitants, their related problems over against the Bantu peoples in their midst and on their borders were ties that were bound to grow stronger with time. But the imperialists could not wait for time to do its work. The Union of South Africa

was to be consummated and the British Empire enlarged in their day, by their hand and on their terms.

The worst outcome of the Raid was that it interrupted the natural growth of unity in South Africa. In 1894 the two white groups were closer together politically in the Cape than they had ever been and the Orange Free State was linked with the South in a customs and railway union. After the Raid those bonds parted. Hofmeyr and the Cape Afrikaners broke their connection with the English federalists. The Orange Free State withdrew into a political alliance with the Transvaal. South African politics started on a new course determined by ties of kinship and language that cut across the geographical and economic unity of the country.

Yet it was less the Raid itself that had these consequences than the attempt to free the Imperial authorities of all responsibility for it. No one can say with certainty what would have happened if their complicity had been admitted. Some of those who took it upon themselves to be silent predicted a war between Great Britain and Germany, even a European war, as the outcome of such an admission. This prediction, however sincerely made, had no foundation. All the evidence on the state of mind of the German Government at the time goes to show that it would never have encouraged, still less actively supported, the Transvaal in any serious defiance of Great Britain, however strong the moral and legal position of the Republic may have been. Germany was not prepared in 1896 to wage a war in which naval superiority must have been the decisive factor. France and Russia were unwilling to join her even in a tweaking of the lion's tail. And the Transvaal would hardly have attacked alone. It was inadequately armed in 1896, and if the wrong done to it had been acknowledged, it would have been morally disarmed as well.

On the other hand it is almost certain that an admission of complicity would have forced Chamberlain to resign in 1896, perhaps even to retire from public life; and that might well have changed the course of South African history. The Conservative Government, losing its most powerful minister on such an issue, must then have gone to the country, as it did in 1905 after Chamberlain left the Cabinet; and if the Liberals had won the 1906 election ten years earlier, the imperialists might have been curbed. The Anglo-Boer War might never have been fought and the South African states and colonies might have been left to accomplish amicably and in due time a federation from within.

If its history had taken such a course, South Africa might to-day have possessed a slowly-matured federal constitution instead of an artificially constructed union that had to fit the extraordinary conditions created by the defeat of the Republics and by the need to integrate them quickly, yet securely, into a self-governing British Dominion. There is not much doubt that such a federation would have been able to accommodate the differences between the four provinces, particularly the race and colour differences, far better than the present close union has been able to do and that it would have allowed diversity and freedom in many fields where now only a restricting uniformity is possible.

But, above all, South Africa might have been spared the legacy of what was really a civil war. The passions born of such conflicts die hard. In South Africa they have had the effect of retarding the growth of a common nationhood and of weakening and distracting its people in their approach to the problems of their undeveloped and racially complex country. The shielding of Chamberlain had much to do with the coming of war. It left a determined, and temporarily discomfited, imperialist in power. And it aroused in the minds of the Afrikaners a deep suspicion of the Government that he dominated. In such circumstances the negotiations that preceded the war could not be conducted soberly and generously. They were vitiated from the start.

When one looks back at this episode in the history of imperialist expansion, it seems that no great harm would have been done and that the worst consequences of the Raid might have been avoided if there had been a frank avowal of the part played in it by the Imperial authorities, and if the responsible minister and his party had then suffered the ordinary constitutional penalties. When the opposite course was taken, a tragic error was made.

IV. THE CLASH OF OPINION
IN BRITAIN, 1899

The "battle of the journalists" which was waged over imperial policy in 1899 was marked by the most vigorous expression of views on both sides. The readings in this section are by two men of outstanding intellectual and literary attainments who held diametrically opposed views on the policy in South Africa. Curiously, they had been collaborators for a number of years. Edward Tyas Cook (1857–1919) was one of the most influential London journalists in the closing years of the nineteenth century. From 1883 to 1890 he served on the staff of the *Pall Mall Gazette*, a liberal organ, then edited by W. T. Stead. Serving for a time on the same paper was Alfred Milner, later the High Commissioner in South Africa, but then engaged in his brief career in journalism. These three men formed a remarkable trio. Cook succeeded Stead as editor of the *Gazette* in 1890, and then became editor, successively, of the *Westminster Gazette* (which he founded) and of the *Daily News*. His considerable scholarly reputation stemmed from his biographies of Ruskin and of *Delane*, of *The Times*. His rejection of "little Englandism" brought him into conflict with many in the Liberal Party. He remained an admirer of Milner and the most able exponent of Milner's work in South Africa. In the first reading below, Cook sets forth his reasons for believing in a Boer plan to end British paramountcy in South Africa.

Cook's views were opposed in 1899 by his erstwhile chief, William Thomas Stead (1849–1912). After gaining an outstanding reputation as editor of the *Pall Mall Gazette*, Stead resigned in 1890 to found his *Review of Reviews*, of which he remained editor for many years. Rejecting the imperialism of Milner and Cook, Stead wrote numerous articles and tracts which established him as the most uncompromising of all critics of the Government's policy in South Africa. He died in the Titanic disaster, 1912.

A Far Ranging Boer Conspiracy

E. T. COOK

IN a manifesto issued by Mr. Courtney it is stated that "the so-called Dutch conspiracy to oust British power from South Africa rests on the most shadowy foundation." If the controversy is to be made to turn on the word "conspiracy," I should be inclined to agree with Mr. Courtney. I have never seen evidence to show that there was a definitely formulated conspiracy between the two Republics on the one side and prominent Dutch colonists on the other to oust British power from South Africa. The conclusion suggested by a study of South African history points rather to a conflict of tendencies, of ideals, of ambitions. The principle of British policy in South Africa in relation to the Transvaal was local autonomy for that State, protected, however, and controlled in its foreign policy by Great Britain. The principle of Transvaal policy was very different. Its ambition was to become an absolutely independent and sovereign State, constantly enlarging its borders and throwing off daughter Republics; so that when the time came for the formation of the United South Africa aimed at by the Afrikander Bond, the paramount power should be that, not of Great Britain, but of the Dutch Republics.

What has been suggested is, then, that the Transvaal Government was resolved to be rid of the last vestiges of British supremacy; that the Orange Free State had been induced to sympathize with them in this object; that an ideal widely held amongst the Boers was a United States of South Africa, under a Boer flag; that this ideal was cherished by an extreme wing of the Afrikander Bond; and that the Republican propaganda had many adherents among the Dutch subjects of the Crown. This is the rational and historical form of the theory referred to by Mr. Courtney. In this form the statement, so far from having no foundation in fact, is in some measure open to no question whatever; and the assertion, often made, that the theory was an "afterthought" on the British side is demonstrably incorrect. It was placed on record by Lord Milner in a despatch which preceded the negotiations of 1899, and it had been put forth many years before by other men, whose knowledge of South Africa was wide, and whose freedom from bias against the Boers is beyond question.

The first clause in the series of propositions set out above — the statement that the Transvaal Government aimed at complete independence of Great Britain — admits of no sort of doubt. The essential documents to study in this connection are in the Blue-Book of 1884 containing "Correspondence respecting the Convention concluded with the South African Republic on the 27th February, 1884." The first thing which will strongly impress the reader is the view put forward by Mr. Kruger of the Convention of 1881. We in this country are in the habit of speaking of Mr. Gladstone's policy therein as a piece of extraordinary magnanimity. To Mr. Kruger, on the other hand, the boot was on the other leg. "The said Convention," he remarks, "was only ratified by the Volksraad under compulsion to prevent further bloodshed." What Mr. Kruger specially objected to was that the Convention was "a unilateral document framed by a Royal Commission," and that the Transvaal did not have "the status of a contracting party."

Accordingly, what he asked for was that the status established by the Convention of

From E. T. Cook, *Rights and Wrongs of the Transvaal War,* new and revised edition (London: Edward Arnold, 1902), pp. 18–23; 266–267; 276–279; 281–282.

1881 should be altered by a new instrument founded on the basis of "two contracting Powers." Here we find the first germ of that claim to the status of a Sovereign International State which Mr. Kruger and his advisers never henceforth for a moment abandoned, which governed their policy for two decades, and which was to play so large and fatal a part in producing the rupture of 1899. In the draft *treaty* submitted by Mr. Kruger and his fellow-delegates on November 26, 1883, care was taken, both in its form and in its substance, to embody the claim to be a Sovereign International State. We need not, however, here examine the draft, though hereafter we shall have to recur to it in other connections; for Lord Derby promptly replied that the treaty was "neither in form nor in substance such as Her Majesty's Government could adopt." The actual Convention ultimately agreed to contained, as everybody knows, at least one article which was obviously inconsistent with the status of a Sovereign International State. This was Article IV., under which treaties negotiated by the South African Republic were reserved for the approval of Her Majesty the Queen. Mr. Kruger signed that article. Did he thereby renounce his claim? Not at all. This is a subject on which strange misrepresentations have been made by Mr. Kruger's friends. He accepted the Convention of 1884, indeed, but he accepted it only as an instalment. Like a certain section of the Irish Nationalists, he might accept compromises, but his real aim was to sever "the last link."

*   *   *

The Convention of 1884 limited the Transvaal's ambitions in two ways. It placed the Republic in a position of semi-dependence on Great Britain; and it strictly shut it off from encroachments beyond its borders. Just as President Kruger set himself to abrogate the Convention in the former respect, so also he attempted unceasingly, and in all quarters of the compass, to violate it in the latter respect. The first attempt was made on the west, in the hope of securing control over the great trade route northward. This was stopped by Mr. Gladstone when he sent out Sir Charles Warren's expedition and proclaimed the Bechuanaland Protectorate in 1885. The next attempt to violate the Convention was made in the years 1889, 1890, 1891, when it was hoped to forestall Mr. Rhodes in Mashonaland. To these attempts we shall return in a later chapter. On the complicated story of President Kruger's ambitions eastwards — that is, seawards — the *Quarterly* reviewer gives a very lucid account of Lord Loch's negotiations. Her Majesty's Government, steadily pursuing a policy of conciliation, not only surrendered Swaziland, but offered President Kruger a seaport. There were, however, the following conditions, among others, attached: that the Republic should not, without the approval of Her Majesty's Government, part with the harbour, or enter into any treaty regarding it; and that if any dispute arose with a Foreign Power regarding the harbour, the diplomatic negotiations should be carried on by Her Majesty's Government. President Kruger, who had previously enlarged on the commercial importance of a seaport, declined these conditions. Can any reasonable doubt exist as to his motives? The President tried threats; the concessions obtained for him on the sea-coast might be transferred to some Foreign Power. He also tried intrigues; and in the end Lord Ripon, on the advice of Lord Loch, annexed the territories in question to Zululand. The whole story makes it abundantly clear that the real object of the President, in his eastward extension schemes, was to take another step towards the complete independence of the Republic. To quote the reviewer again: "What the Government of Pretoria aimed at was an extension of territory which, had it been granted, would have made the Republic the leading and dominant State in South Africa. On the west they tried to secure the control over the great trade route northward; on the north they coveted the territories of the

Matabele and of the Mashona; on the east they claimed that all the country which lay between the Republic and the sea should be surrendered to them, so that, with a harbour and a sea-coast of their own, they might take their place as a completely independent State in the family of nations." All this is not a matter of argument, but a matter of fact.

*   *   *

In England many people pictured Mr. Kruger and the Boers as quaking in their shoes at the idea of a rupture, or as solemnly taking up a forlorn hope. Very different was the impression made upon visitors to Pretoria. "The Pretoria people," wrote Sir Henry de Villiers to his brother, "do not seem to realize the position. When I was there, Reitz seemed to treat the whole matter as a big joke." Other people have pictured the Boers as taking up arms, not gladly though resolutely, in defence of their hearths and homes. The following extract from a letter written by a member of the Transvaal Volksraad to a member of the Legislative Assembly of Cape Colony puts matters in a somewhat different light:

Our plan is, with God's help, to take all that is English in South Africa, so, in case you true Afrikaners wish to throw off the English yoke, now is the time to hoist the Vierkleur in Cape Town. You can rely on us; we will push through from sea to sea, and wave one flag over the whole of South Africa under one Afrikander Government, if we can reckon on our Afrikander brethren.

*   *   *

When war was on the eve of breaking out, Canon Farmer, of Pretoria, prepared to take his departure. The Chief Justice (Mr. Gregorowski) tried to dissuade him. "Is it really necessary for you to go?" he asked. "The war will be over in a fortnight. We shall take Kimberley and Mafeking, and give the English such a beating in Natal that they will sue for peace." The testimony of many other South African residents is to like effect. The Boers were

convinced that they would easily be able to "drive the English into the sea." "To get to the sea," said Mr. Schreiner in the Cape Parliament, "was the life and hope of President Kruger." The "young blood" among the burghers in the two Republics had made sure of an easy victory, and the only thing they were afraid of, on the eve of hostilities, was "that Chamberlain, with his admitted fitfulness of temper, would cheat them out of the war, and, consequently, the opportunity of annexing the Cape Colony and Natal, and forming the Republican United States of South Africa." At the outbreak of war such hopes could not have seemed extravagant.

*   *   *

In the days before the war, visitors to Pretoria often described the spectacle of the old President sitting on the stoop with one hand on the Bible and another on the marble lions, the gift of the late Mr. Barnato, which guarded his portals. The picture was typical of the man. He believed in God, but he believed also in force. He put his faith in Maxims no less than in texts, in Krupp and Creuzot as well as in Heaven.

We have discussed already the question when Mr. Kruger began to arm. We saw that the policy of armaments was antecedent to the Raid, but that it was greatly extended after that event, which gave to it some sort of colourable excuse. The point to which we have now to direct attention is the extent and strength of the armaments as disclosed by the war. We all know the theory which was once in favour with a certain school of politicians in this country, and which even now occasionally appears in speeches and in print. The Boers were a community of "poor herdsmen," requiring, indeed, to be able to protect themselves against the possibility of a native attack, and after the Raid awaking to the necessity of being forearmed against a repetition of that lawless enterprise, but for the rest desiring only to live in peace and quiet within their own borders. How this theory has managed to survive the war I do not know. For what did the outbreak of hostilities show? It was seen immediately that for a nation of poor herdsmen the military equipment of the Boers was singularly complete. As the war went on, the demonstration became more and more effective. The Boers were found to have enormous supplies of small arms and ammunition of all sorts, and a most formidable equipment of heavy artillery. It is not within my province to note the technical questions which have been debated upon this point. At any rate it is agreed that the Boer artillery in some respects outclassed the British. Mr. Kruger had turned the Uitlanders' gold into guns of the very best and latest types, and this, we may suppose, was one of the advantages on which he most counted.

It is idle to suppose that the great armaments of the Transvaal were procured as a protection against the natives or a second Dr. Jameson. The remarks of an ex-Cape Minister in this connection are much to the point. "The Transvaal," he said, "is armed almost like a European Power. Six field-pieces would be adequate for its protection against all the natives who at any time could threaten it. What, then, can it want with fifty, sixty, or eighty modern Krupp guns of the best type? . . . The rapid march of events has compelled them to throw off the mask without further delay. This is fortunate for us, because otherwise we might have had to face two hundred guns instead of sixty or eighty."

The simple truth is that the Transvaal, so far from being a pastoral or industrial State, had converted itself into a huge arsenal, and the only arsenal, be it remembered, in South Africa. There are leagues in these days "against militarism." There is abundant work for them to do, but they neglected a great opportunity in not addressing their protests to Pretoria. South Africa, secured from foreign aggression by the navy of the Paramount Power, was a country from which the curse of militarism should and could have been banished. Its internal conditions called for nothing but

such arms as might be necessary to guard against native risings. It is a country of great resources which cry out for peaceful development by the joint efforts of the two white races to whom its destinies are committed. In the British colonies and protectorates complete equality of opportunity was granted to Dutch and British and all white races alike. In British South Africa the garrison in normal times consisted of no more than a couple of regiments of cavalry and five battalions of infantry. It was the Transvaal, the peaceful Arcadia of imaginative politicians, that introduced militarism into South Africa. By railing off a huge tract of territory as a reserve for the political ascendancy of one race, Mr. Kruger sowed the seeds of discord. Mr. Rhodes and Dr. Jameson completed the evil by a resort to force which gave Mr. Kruger his excuse, and the "Arcadia" was turned into an arsenal.

Against whom was it directed? It must have been, it could only have been, directed against England. As Mr. Lecky says, the Transvaal "raised an annual revenue greatly in excess of what was required for its internal government from unrepresented Engglishmen, to whom the prosperity of the State was mainly due, and it employed that revenue in accumulating a great armament which could only be intended for use against England. The events of the last months have shown that it had become incomparably the most powerful State in South Africa, and that if we had been engaged in a serious European war the English colonies would have been at its mercy."

*　　*　　*

We have seen that ever since 1881 a hostile policy towards England was unswervingly pursued by the Transvaal. Ceaseless attempts were made, in some cases successfully, to violate the conditions on which Mr. Gladstone had restored the internal independence of the Republic. Claims were put forward in the negotiations of 1883 which showed the ultimate ambitions of the Transvaal. The English inhabitants of the country were disfranchised; they were unrepresented, but they were taxed, and the money was used to convert the Republic into a powerful military State, and at the same time to provide for a large expenditure in Secret Service, both in Europe and in Africa. The war has revealed to us on the Transvaal side a formidable combination of military equipment, complete organization, experienced tactics, and a vast accumulation of artillery and ammunition. This combination was thrown by the two Boer States into an invasion of the British colonies, after they had refused terms which their most ardent defenders in this country admitted to be reasonable and conciliatory, and after the British Government had offered, if those terms were accepted, "to give a complete guarantee against any attack upon the independence of the South African Republic, either from within any part of the British dominions, or from the territory of any foreign State."

Is it possible on this collocation of facts to resist the conclusion that the final declaration of war was the culmination of a determined policy, deliberately planned and strenuously pursued?

How the British Government Caused the War

W. T. STEAD

THE British public last month experienced a somewhat unusual sensation. Everybody is acquainted with the most familiar of all Æsop's fables, the Wolf and the Lamb, but everyone has hitherto, without exception, read that apologue from the point of view of the lamb. For the first time in the lives of many they were last month able to put themselves in the place of the wolf, and curiously enough they seem to have come to the conclusion that the wolf has not only a great deal to say for himself, but that the devouring of the lamb was the imperative and painful duty which no wolf with any respect for the law of man or God could avoid. The difficulty of putting oneself in another's place was seldom more conspicuously manifested. We are now able to fill in many details in the fable which old Æsop left out. Probably if he had written out all the facts, we should have found that immediately before devouring the lamb, the wolf said grace before meat, and that after he had finished he, as piously, thanked God for having rewarded his faithful servant.

*   *   *

The story of our dealings with the Transvaal in the last few weeks displayed all the familiar characteristics of the dealings of the wolf with the lamb. Its chief characteristic has constantly been shifting the ground for quarrel whenever it seemed likely that our victim would escape. In the month of August it seemed likely that the difference was about to be arranged. The Transvaal Government, under pressure of the "friendly counsels" of Sir Alfred Milner and the more urgent representations of the Cape Dutch, had reduced their franchise from fourteen years to seven, and enacted a law by which any Outlander who could prove that he has lived seven years in the Transvaal would at once be enrolled as a burgher, and would be entitled to vote for the Volksraad and for the appointment of the President and the commandant general. Mr. Chamberlain publicly declared that this offered a basis of settlement, and proposed that a mixed commission should be appointed to place beyond all doubt the satisfactory character of the seven years' franchise law of July. As President Kruger is said to have declared that the seven years' franchise law would emancipate fifty thousand Outlanders — that is to say, nearly twice the number of the old Boers on the electoral roll — all that appeared to be necessary was a local Commission of Inquiry to verify on the spot the justice of the President's anticipations. Owing to some conversation between the State's Attorney, Mr. Smuts, and the British Agent, Mr. Conyngham Greene, President Kruger got it into his head that if he offered five years' franchise he might be able to secure from the British Government a definite repudiation of all right to interfere in the Transvaal by virtue of the suzerainty of 1881 which they believed had been abandoned in 1884, but which Mr. Chamberlain had revived in his despatch of October, 1897. There were other conditions, but this was the vital point upon which they insisted. President Kruger then made a definite offer that in exchange for the repudiation of all right to interfere in the internal affairs of the Transvaal by virtue of the suzerainty of 1881 he would concede the five years' franchise. This offer was made in August, in the confident anticipation that it would

From *Review of Reviews*, London edition, ed. W. T. Stead (October, 1899), pp. 329–333.

be gladly accepted, and that the controversy would be closed. To their astonishment and dismay the offer was rejected, the suzerainty was reaffirmed, and all that was stated about arbitration was that the British Government was willing to discuss the matter.

On September 2nd the Boers, finding their offer rejected, fell back upon the old proposal of our Government, and in somewhat involved terms assented to the proposed Commission of Inquiry into the seven years' franchise. Thereupon the Cabinet decided to abandon their old ground of inquiry by mixed commission into the seven years' franchise, declared that they were satisfied that the seven years' franchise would not give immediate and substantial representation to the Outlanders, and then demanded that President Kruger should give the five years' franchise. They added a new demand that English should be admitted equally with Dutch in the discussions of the Volksraad. This despatch, by a miracle of self-deception, was declared in this country to be a marvel of moderation and patience. In reality it simply asked the Boers to give the five years' franchise while refusing to grant the *quid pro quo* which the Boers required. As the *quid pro quo* merely consisted of a request that we should formally agree to keep our pledged word, abandon the mendacious pretension that the suzerainty of 1881 was still in existence, and refer disputes to arbitration, it is difficult to see, excepting from the standpoint of the wolf, where the moderation comes in. On September 16th the Boers replied, expressing their surprise that a new proposal should have been sprung upon them after they had accepted the original proposition of Mr. Chamberlain to refer the seven years' franchise to a mixed commission of inquiry. They also remarked somewhat drily that "it is not clear on what grounds Her Majesty's Government, after having recently, by means of its invitation intimated that it could not declare without an inquiry whether the franchise law would afford immediate and

substantial representation, is to-day, without having made any inquiry, in a position to declare that the measure thus mentioned is insufficient for the object contemplated." They therefore renewed their acceptance of the proposed Mixed Commission, and while repudiating any promise to allow English to be used in the Volksraad, expressed an earnest hope that the Government would refrain from springing fresh demands upon them, and would declare itself satisfied to abide by its own proposal for a joint commission, which Mr. Chamberlain had proposed, and which they had accepted. This despatch was the pitiful bleat of the lamb, and quite as unanswerable in its way as the famous rejoinder of its prototype in Æsop's fable. Alas, the wolf answered after its kind!

*   *   *

They have launched another despatch to the Boers in which they renewed their demand for the five years' franchise, and instead of abandoning the preposterous claim to interfere on the ground of the suzerainty of 1881, offered the Boers a guarantee against outside attack which they did not ask for, and the value of which, coming from the hero of the South Africa Committee, could hardly be regarded as worth the paper it was written on. The offer, unasked for, of protection seemed to foreign observers to be an insidious method of asserting a protectorate which in the nature of things would entail much more control over their foreign policy than we have at present. The Transvaal, although technically not a Sovereign International State, inasmuch as it cannot make treaties without submitting them to our veto, is nevertheless sovereign and international to this extent, that it can make war if it pleases, and carry out any kind of foreign policy so long as it does not embody its decision not to do so in a treaty with any foreign Power. But, if once the Transvaal accepted our undertaking to protect it from foreign attack, it would give us in a very practical fashion a right to control its conduct, otherwise the Transvaal might land us in a war at any time by any act of mad folly or reckless ambition. As if to emphasise the fact that Ministers had no intention of honestly recognising the independence of the little republic, Mr. Chamberlain contrived to insert in the despatch a sinister reference to the obligations of the Transvaal under the "Conventions," a use of the plural number which the Boers at once interpreted as a decisive rejection of their plea for the abandonment of the suzerainty of 1881. Thus refusing what they asked for, and offering them the fatal gift of protectorate instead, we reiterated our demands for the concession of the five years' franchise.

*   *   *

The Boers were in no hurry to reply to the last despatch of the British Government. That missive concluded with the threat that if the reply was unsatisfactory to us we would once more change the issue and, abandoning all discussion of the franchise upon which we had hitherto insisted, would proceed to formulate other demands not particularly specified, but which it was clearly understood would entail direct interference on our part in the internal affairs of the Transvaal. In other words, if the Boers did not do what we asked them to do we would at once proceed to do what we had promised them we would not do. This is only one more illustration of the continual shifting of the issue by our Government. The Ministerial Press, however, and the Ministerial eulogists on the platform are now proclaiming that the issue is to be changed once more. Instead of demanding the inquiry into the five years' franchise which has already been offered them if we would abandon the suzerainty of 1881, or the detailed series of reforms which are not yet formulated, all those questions which have been put up as stalking-horses to conceal the real question at issue are to be thrown overboard, and we are to go to war with the Transvaal solely upon the question of asserting our supremacy or paramountcy in South Africa.

Considering that no one has questioned this, and that, as Mr. Garrett points out in an article quoted elsewhere, it is based, in the nature of things, upon the overwhelming balance of forces, industrial, financial, and numerical, in South Africa, we have as little need to go to war to assert it as the wolf did to eat the lamb, merely in order to prove that he had stronger teeth. Of all the disreputable, contemptible, and discreditable proceedings by which a nation has ever been jockeyed into war, this fighting for the paramountcy is about the worst. The wolf in the fable at least shrank from the effrontery of pretending to be frightened of the lamb; but here we have persons presumably sane proclaiming that we are face to face with a deadly plot on the part of the Dutch in South Africa to destroy our authority, and to establish a great Dutch Republic on the ruins of the British Empire in South Africa.

V. CAUSED BY JINGOISM?

The term "jingoism" became part of the English vocabulary as a result of the Balkan crisis of 1878, when the war spirit in England gave rise to the popular song:

> "We don't want to fight;
> But by Jingo, if we do,
> We've got the men, we've got the ships,
> We've got the money too."

Twenty years later the term was frequently used to describe the super-patriotism and war spirit which was fostered by those supporting imperialism. The reading below is from the book by J. A. Hobson, *The Psychology of Jingoism*. Written as a follow-up to his book of the preceding year, *The War in South Africa, Its Causes and Effects*, it is a further blast at the government's policy. Hobson analyzes the state of mind called jingoism and develops his thesis as to the factors which created this spirit.

The Forces of Press, Platform, and Pulpit

J. A. HOBSON

A recent French writer, discoursing on the nature of "a crowd," attributes to it a character and conduct which is lower, intellectually and morally, than the character and conduct of its average member. Even when the crowd is little other than a fortuitous concourse, and not an organized gathering of persons already assimilated by some common feeling or idea, a sort of common mind is temporarily set up, which often seems to dominate, or even to supersede, the normal mind of the individual. A sensational rumour, a sudden unusual spectacle, the powerful appeal of a mob orator, so agitates the mass of individuals, hitherto related by mere propinquity, as to raise, by a largely unconscious interaction of personalities, a quick ferment of thought and feeling which impels individuals to take part in a common action that is not their mere individual choice. This passion of the mob, implying an abandonment of self-control by the individual, is a fact too well recognized to require proof. But its nature and origin are both obscure and interesting. This war in South Africa casts a powerful searchlight upon the nature of the large, and in some ways highly-organized, crowd which we call the British nation. The suddenness, the size, and the manifold sensationalism of the occurrence are the precise conditions requisite for testing the mass-mind of the people. What the orator does for his audience the press has done for the nation; it has injected notions and feelings which, instead of lying in the separate minds of their recipients, have bubbled up into enthusiastic sympathy, and induced a community of thought, language, and action which was hitherto unknown.

* * *

Now, the most astonishing phenomenon of this war-fever is the credulity displayed by the educated classes. It is, of course, true that ordinary education is so curiously defective in this country that not one in fifty persons could have correctly named the capital of the Orange Free State at the beginning of 1899. But education might have been expected to teach caution in the acceptance and assimilation of the flood of information which poured through the press during the last two years. Our educated classes are usually scornful of the man who believes everything he reads in the newspapers, and who pronounces quick dogmatic judgments upon delicate and intricate points of politics or economics. Yet the majority of these cultured persons have submitted their intelligence to the dominion of popular prejudice and passion as subserviently as the man in the street, whom they despise. The canons of reasoning which they habitually apply in their business or profession, and in the judgments they form of events and characters, are superseded by the sudden fervour of this strange amalgam of race feeling, animal pugnacity, rapacity, and sporting zest, which they dignify by the name of patriotism.

No one would think of accepting in any ordinary private matter of importance the testimony of interested parties, unchecked and incapable of cross-examination, as sufficient evidence to warrant the spending of his money and the risking of his life. Yet the testimony to the Outlander grievances and the Dutch conspiracy given as the justification of this war is almost entirely of this order. The allegation that

From J. A. Hobson, *The Psychology of Jingoism* (London: G. Richards, 1901), pp. 17–18; 21–22; 25–27; 107–112; 138. Reprinted with the permission of John Baker, Ltd.

the press of South Africa, which has furnished information to the press and people of this country, is owned and controlled by a small, known and named body of mining capitalists and speculators who have openly avowed the gains they hoped to make by this war, is not seriously disputed. Yet persons fully aware of this allow their minds to be swayed by the unanimity of the British testimony from South Africa, as presented by this press and by the politicians who have got their information from the same factory of falsehood.

*   *   *

But the most remarkable example of this corruption is afforded by the adoption of members of the mine-owning confraternity as authoritative advisers on the nature of the war and its settlement. Mr. Fitzpatrick, whose book, "The Transvaal from Within," is accepted as if it were the unbiased statement of a skilled historian who happened to reside in the Transvaal, is a member of the Eckstein firm (the local branch of Wernher, Beit, and Co.), and was one of the leaders in the Johannesburg insurrection of 1895; Mr. Lionel Philipps, whose recommendations on settlement were fully reported in the *Times,* is a partner in the same firm; Mr. Hosken, another widely-read authority, is an importer of mining machinery, an ex-director of the *Transvaal Leader,* a newspaper started in the spring of 1899, to bring matters to the test of battle; while Messrs. Rudd, Hayes, Hammond, Robinson, Farrar, and other men, whose voices resound through the British press, are directors and employés of those leading Rand companies, which have calculated the millions they hope to make from the results of the war. It is reasonable that these men should be heard, but it is not reasonable that their statements of fact and views of policy should be taken as authoritative, while the facts and views set forth, not merely by Dutch Colonists, but by British travellers like Mr. Bryce and Mr. Selous, are treated with contempt.

The unanimous support of the Christian Churches in South Africa is similarly raised into authority by leaving out of account the Dutch Christian Churches, which are, of course, equally unanimous in denouncing the war. It is, indeed, curious that men and women with any knowledge of history should adduce the blessing of the Churches as testimony to the justice of any cause. Where have the priests ever failed to bless a war supported by authority and popular passion?

*   *   *

The most momentous lesson of the war is its revelation of the methods by which a knot of men, financiers and politicians, can capture the mind of a nation, arouse its passion, and impose a policy. It is now seen that freedom of speech, public meeting, and press not merely affords no adequate protection against this danger, but that it is itself menaced and impaired; the system of party, which has heretofore, by providing a free, vigorous, and genuine scrutiny of every important political proposal, been a strong safeguard against all endeavours of a clique or a class to exploit the commonwealth, has broken down under the strain of an attack unprecedented in its vigour and in the skill of its direction.

*   *   *

The information from South Africa which impressed upon the public mind a conviction of the justice and necessity of war, and which aroused and sustained the passion of Jingoism, did not flow freely into the country through many diverse, unconnected channels, as is commonly supposed. The extraordinary agreement of the metropolitan and provincial press, Unionist and Liberal, religious and secular, in its presentation of leading facts, in its diagnosis of the situation and its pressure of a drastic policy, is doubtless responsible for the unwavering confidence which the great majority of the nation placed in the policy of the Government at the outset of the war. Such an amount of consentaneity seemed to attest a case of overwhelming strength. When the Government press was joined by the two leading Opposition organs in London, and by the great majority of important Opposition papers throughout the country; when the nonpolitical press, and, in particular, the most powerful journals of the Churches, urged the necessity of war, the doubts of intellect and qualms of conscience in many minds were overborne by such unanimity.

When to this union of the press was added the voices of a thousand pulpits and the instruction of a thousand platforms, where travellers, missionaries, politicians, and philanthropists set forth substantially the same body of facts and drew the same morals, the case for war seemed undeniable.

It is little wonder that people unacquainted with the structure of the press, and with methods of educating public opinion, should have been imposed upon by this concurrence of testimony. If the papers which they read, and the speakers to whom they listened, had drawn their facts and their opinions from a variety of independent sources, the authority they exercised would have been legitimate. But what was the actual case? Turn first to the press, by far the most potent instrument in the modern manufacture of public opinion. The great majority of provincial newspapers, and most of the weeklies, metropolitan or provincial, religious as well as political, derive their information regarding foreign and colonial affairs entirely from the chief London "dailies," supplemented, in the case of the more important organs, by "cables" from the same sources which supply the London "dailies." Most provincial papers take not only their news but their "views," with abject servility, from the London journal which they most admire.

In a very few instances, important provincial papers receive first-hand intelligence from special correspondents of their own by mail, but for all prompt intelligence they are absolutely dependent upon the sources above-mentioned. The otherwise miraculous agreement of the British press is, thus, first resolved into the agreement of a few journals, chiefly in London, and of two or three press agencies. We have next to ask from what sources do these latter get their information? On this point the case of the South African war is peculiarly instructive. All the leading London papers received their South African intelligence from correspondents who were members of the staff of newspapers in Capetown and Johannesburg, supplemented in two instances last year by information from special travelling correspondents, who, in their turn, derived most of that information from newspaper offices in South Africa. In particular, the two London newspapers which exercised most influence upon the mind of the educated classes in this country, the *Times* and the *Daily News,* were instructed, in the former case, by the newly-appointed editor of the Johannesburg *Star,* in the latter case by the editor of the *Cape Times.* The two chief cable companies also drew most of the Capetown intelligence from the *Cape Times* and the *Argus* Company, while one of them was fed with Transvaal intelligence by a prominent member of the Executive of the South African League at Johannesburg.

The press unanimity in Great Britain is thus traced to certain newspaper offices in Capetown and Johannesburg. Now, if these half dozen newspapers had been independent and reliable organs, the news they supplied, and the forcible policy they imposed upon the British press and the British public might have reasonably carried weight. But they were neither independent nor reliable; they are members of a bought and kept press. The *Cape Argus,* bought some years ago by Messrs. Rhodes, Barnato, and Eckstein, is now the nucleus of a Company, owning some half dozen papers in South Africa, and among them the *Star* of Johannesburg, whose editor instructed the readers of the London *Times* in the necessity of war. Since the capture of the Orange Free State, the Company has strengthened its resources by obtaining from the British military authorities the sole right to establish a newspaper at Bloemfontein. The newspapers at Kimberley and at Buluwayo are in the same hands, and the *Cape Times* is financially controlled by Mr. Rutherford Harris, a colleague of Mr. Rhodes in his several financial ventures. The principal organs of public opinion at all the political pivots in South Africa are thus owned by the little group of men who also own or control the diamond mines at Kimberley, the goldfields of the Rand, and the government and resources of Rhodesia.

*   *   *

This conjunction of the forces of the press, the platform, and the pulpit, has succeeded in monopolizing the mind of the British public, and in imposing a policy calculated not to secure the interests of the British Empire, but to advance the private, political, and business interests of a small body of men who have exploited the race feeling in South Africa and the Imperialist sentiment of England. They have done this by the simple device of securing all important avenues of intelligence, and of using them to inject into the public mind a continuous stream of false or distorted information.

VI. A WAR TO PRESERVE
THE BRITISH EMPIRE?

In the past thirty years the tendency among historians has been to interpret the Anglo-Boer War, at least in terms of British policy, as essentially a war for the Empire. This by no means implies that Britain was the aggressor or that the war was primarily one for imperial expansion. In fact, two of the historians who are quoted in this section present arguments in support of official British policy. The first reading is by R. C. K. Ensor, from his work *England 1870–1914*, previously quoted in connection with the Jameson Raid. Although he points out mistakes in the conduct of British diplomacy, Ensor views the policy of war as essentially defensive, a policy which the government had little choice but to follow in view of the obstructionist and aggressive elements in "Krugerism."

The second reading in this section is by the American historian, Professor C. W. de Kiewiet, president of the University of Rochester from 1951 to 1962 and a specialist on South African history. His best known works are *The Imperial Factor in South Africa* (1937) and *A History of South Africa, Social and Economic* (1941), from which the selection here is taken. Professor de Kiewiet emphasizes the liberal and constructive aspects of British policy, which had long aimed at a selfgoverning and federated South Africa within the Commonwealth.

The third reading is by William L. Langer, for many years Professor of History at Harvard University and author of a number of works in the field of diplomatic history. His two-volume study, *The Diplomacy of Imperialism, 1890–1902*, published in 1935, made use of the great body of historical materials which had become available to scholars up to that time—biographies, personal memoirs, and official papers, as well as periodical literature of the period preceding the war. Professor Langer examines critically the various theories of causation which had been advanced since 1899, and he presents an analysis of the diplomatic negotiations between the governments of Great Britain and the South African Republic in the years 1896–1899. In conclusion he suggests that a good deal of the responsibility for war must be assigned to the policies advanced by Milner and Chamberlain.

The final two readings in this section bear witness to the intensive research conducted since 1945 by scholars who have gained access to significant sources of information hitherto unavailable for study. Of these the Chamberlain papers are perhaps the most important, but much revealing information has also been found in government archives and in the personal papers of other leading personalities in England and South Africa. The book by Ronald Robinson and John Gallagher, with Alice Denny, *Africa and the Victorians: The Official Mind of Imperialism* (1961), approaches the subject, not from the standpoint of economic and social forces, nor of general theories of imperialism, but rather with a view to discovering the rationale of policy which existed in the minds of officials who guided British policy. By a close examination of official memoranda and letters, the authors create a picture of policy in the making. The authors are historians at the University of Cambridge.

The final reading in this section is by the South African historian, J. S. Marais, Professor of History at the University of the Witwatersrand. His work, *The Fall of Kruger's Republic* (1961), constitutes the most detailed study of factors leading to the war which has thus far appeared, and it has been referred to as a "model of historical scholarship." The reading presented here is his chapter entitled "Conclusion."

The Whole Future of the Dominions Was Concerned

R. C. K. ENSOR

WE must turn back to South Africa, which during the lifetime of this government was never far out of the picture. In March 1897 Sir Hercules Robinson (who had become Lord Rosmead) was recalled, and a new high commissioner sent. This was Sir Alfred Milner, who till then had been chairman of the Board of Inland Revenue. When not in an official position he had always been a liberal; but his experience in Egypt, where he took part in a most beneficent phase of British rule under Lord Cromer, had made him also a convinced imperialist. He went to South Africa with the good wishes of all parties, and not least of the Opposition. Yet in one respect his was not a good appointment. He had the gifts and temperament of a first-class administrator. But he lacked those of a diplomatist.

Just before he started, a conflict had developed with Kruger over two new and tyrannical aliens laws, whose repeal Chamberlain demanded. The president was not ready to fight, and he gave way. But he spent the year arming. The war material imported through Delagoa Bay rose from £61,903, in 1895 to £256,291 in 1897. Over £1½ millions was spent on forts at Johannesburg; heavy guns were mounted, and German artillery officers engaged. Over £70,000 was allocated for the secret service maintained by the Transvaal in the adjoining British territories. Asked in August by the prime minister of Natal what was the motive of his enormous armaments, Kruger replied: "Oh, Kaffirs, Kaffirs—and such-like objects."

Milner spent his first ten months studying the situation. He travelled over the colonies, learned Dutch, and saw every one that he could. Much would depend on the Transvaal presidential election in February 1898. As we have seen, it resulted overwhelmingly in Kruger's favour. The old man followed up his triumph by trampling on the Transvaal judicature, dismissing its head, and making himself virtually a dictator. Milner, the workings of whose mind may be traced almost from day to day in the *Milner Papers,* now became deeply alarmed. He wrote to Chamberlain that "there is no way out of the political troubles of South Africa except reform in the Transvaal or war. And at present the chances of reform in the Transvaal are worse than ever." In a notable speech at Graaff-Reinet (1 March) he warned the Cape Dutch that the cause of strife lay not in the British policy but in Krugerism, and they must exert their influence against the latter if they desired peace. He obtained but a limited response. What above all kept the Dutch aloof was the re-emergence of Rhodes. The "Colossus," though fallen from his ministerial pedestal, was too big a personality not to have resumed unofficially the leadership of the British element in South Africa. But all sections of Dutch opinion combined now in an invincible distrust of him; and when, for instance, on his return after the Raid Inquiry he gave out his slogan: "Equal rights for all civilized men south of the Zambesi," the effect was to render suspect a claim whose justice more than half of them would otherwise support. In April 1898 he recovered his place on the board of the Chartered Company, which Chamberlain in 1896 had forced him to resign.

From R. C. K. Ensor, *England 1870–1914,* Vol. XIV of *The Oxford History of England,* ed. G. N. Clark (Oxford, 1936), pp. 245–251. Reprinted by permission of The Clarendon Press, Oxford.

As 1898 wore on, another hope appeared. There was a chance that by an arrangement with Portugal and Germany, Great Britain might acquire Delagoa Bay. It was assumed (though in the light of what we now know it seems very doubtful) that, if this happened, the Transvaal would accept the completion of its encirclement without fighting. But it fell through. At the Cape elections in the autumn the Sprigg ministry, which had succeeded Rhodes's, was defeated by the Dutch party, the "Bond." A ministry was formed under W. P. Schreiner, himself a moderate man of high ideals, but entirely dependent on the votes of extremists (14 October 1898).

In November Milner went home on leave, and during his absence an event occurred at Johannesburg which incalculably increased the tension. An English workman, one Tom Edgar, was shot dead by a Boer policeman in circumstances which Uitlander opinion (quite justly, on the reported facts) regarded as constituting murder. The policeman was arrested, released on nominal bail, tried for manslaughter two months later before a jury of Boers, and not merely acquitted, but commended by the presiding judge. This episode transformed the character of the Uitlander unrest. Hitherto it had been controlled by the capitalists. Now a mass agitation ran away with the workmen; and the harsh violence which the Boers proceeded to use towards it only increased its momentum. A petition from British subjects on the Rand to the queen received 21,684 signatures in a few weeks. It was sent home on 24 March; and when it reached Downing Street the government faced a sharp dilemma. Either they must take it up; which, if Kruger persisted in flat defiance, might mean war. Or they must decline it; which would mean notifying all loyal British subjects in South Africa, and indeed overseas generally, that the mother country washed her hands of them. They delayed decision for several weeks, but on 9 May they took up the petition. They were no doubt stiffened by the famous "helots" dispatch from Milner, which had reached them a few days earlier giving chapter and verse for the Uitlanders' grievances.

The full details of negotiation between this point and the outbreak of hostilities five months later are too intricate to be traced here. New light on them has been thrown by quite recent publications. The effect of these has been to dispel the myth that a bellicose Chamberlain drove a reluctant cabinet into war. The documents show that the cabinet was indeed reluctant, but so was the colonial secretary. He had, as we shall see later on, been taking a leading part in European affairs, and was fully alive to the grave risks of a colonial war-entanglement. Moreover his training as a business man had given him a strong bias towards negotiation. He never failed in patience or diplomatic resource during these months. The person who did was Milner. The high commissioner had made up his mind (and his view cannot be lightly ignored, for he formed it on the spot and was a good judge of facts) that the Transvaal's helm was set for an independent United States of South Africa under Dutch auspices, and that Kruger, with the wind of Afrikanderdom in his sails, was most unlikely to abandon the goal under any pressure short of military defeat. Therefore, while constrained to negotiations by Chamberlain, he did not approach them with hope or zest.

Four stages may be briefly distinguished. The first, after the British government had accepted the Uitlander petition, was a direct conference at Bloemfontein between Milner and Kruger (31 May-5 June 1899). Here was perhaps the best hope of peace, for the moderate Dutch of the Cape and the Free State brought considerable pressure to bear on the Transvaal extremists. But Milner appeared at his worst; his clear super-civilized mind lost patience with the tedious and devious obstinacy of the Arcadian president; and after five days he broke off the talks. A cable from Chamberlain urging him not to, and suggesting new lines of negotiation, reached him just too late. The second stage saw a long discussion of various obscure and complicated franchise bills in the Transvaal legislature, while the Cape Dutch leaders renewed their moderating efforts; until Chamberlain (27 July) offered an olive-branch in the form of a proposal for joint inquiry into the bills by British and Boer delegations. The Dutch in the Cape parliament welcomed this, but Kruger would not listen to them. Then, thirdly, came new and much more liberal proposals, made (13 August) to the British agent through the Transvaal state attorney, Jan Christiaan Smuts. These, as they stood, seemed to end the dispute, but Kruger went on to add conditions which he knew the British government could not accept; and on 2 September he withdrew the offer. The fourth stage consisted of a final offer by Chamberlain in moderate and conciliatory terms (8 September); which, though approved by the Cape Dutch leaders as well as by what were soon to be called the "pro-Boers" in England, was rejected in a few days. A last attempt by Chamberlain (22 September) to keep the door open met with no response. Nor did a conciliatory speech (30 September) by the much-trusted duke of Devonshire. Both sides turned to moving troops.

It must be added that throughout these years a dispute had persisted, first by itself and then as a bitter flavouring in the main discussions, about the word "suzerainty," which was used in the preamble to the 1881 Convention, but not repeated in the Convention of 1884. The British government maintained that the preamble governed both conventions (the second revising the first in respect of its articles only). No less a person than Sir Edward Clarke, solicitor-general in Salisbury's previous government, held this British interpretation to be wrong. But Chamberlain was not pedantic about it; he disclaimed any wish to read into "suzerainty" more than the 1884 Convention itself contained. It is difficult to say how much mischief the

word bred; but Sir Henry (afterwards Lord) de Villiers, the Afrikaner chief justice of the Cape, who worked as hard to save peace as any one, thought that through its effect on Kruger it was of capital importance.

Should the war have been avoided? The liberal party at home became divided between those like Morley who thought so (the "pro-Boers") and those like Lord Rosebery who thought not (the "liberal imperialists"); Campbell-Bannerman inclining to the former camp, and Asquith to the latter. The cleavage rent the party for a long time; but there were eventual compensations. The fact that the "pro-Boers" had been numerous and courageous helped much in the reconciliation of the Transvaal seven years later. The fact, too, that the leaders of the I.L.P. and the young radicals stood together on difficult and unpopular anti-war platforms rendered easier that measure of general co-operation between them which under the Campbell-Bannerman and Asquith governments was fruitful in social reform.

But History, to the question posed above, has since found no certain answer. It is easy to argue after the event that the risks and losses of the long struggle were disproportionate to the Uitlanders' grievances, and that the Transvaal must eventually have reformed itself when Kruger, who was old, should die. But Kruger, even when broken and in exile, lived till 1904; and if Great Britain had left her oppressed nationals unchampioned until then, she might by then have looked in vain for any loyal nationals in South Africa. Much more than the details of the case for redress was involved in her accepting the Uitlander petition. It concerned the whole future of the Dominions, and can only be judged in the light of whatever value we may think that they (and particularly the Union of South Africa) possess, as Dominions, for Great Britain. Probably, however, no government could have let the petition drop. Nor after it was accepted is it easy to see much room for improvement in the British handling, save at the Bloemfontein Conference. Chamberlain worked well, though seriously and undeservedly handicapped by the suspicion of his personality, with which party feeling in England had infected South Africa.

There remain two wider factors. Though the cabinet of Great Britain was not bellicose, a large and noisy section of her people undoubtedly were. London imperialism, in particular, had developed during the nineties a swaggering aggressiveness; it grew markedly worse after the victory of Omdurman. If Jameson had become a hero by atoning for Isandhlwana, what of Kitchener, who had retrieved Khartoum? And what remained to complete the trilogy but to undo Majuba in like fashion? It is often said that this temper caused the war; and it may be true, though not in the most obvious sense. It did not affect Whitehall; the exceedingly strong combination of Salisbury, Chamberlain, Balfour, and Hicks Beach was one much above yielding to mob-clamour. But it did affect Pretoria. If the Boers became united by the mistaken conviction that a British government wanted their blood, it was largely because they heard a British public calling for it.

But secondly, the Boers were not thinking of defence only. There was a strong aggressive element on their side. They had sound military reasons for expecting to win, and but for an early error in large strategy might well have done so. They went into the fight as a new War of Independence, necessary to give birth to a new United States. At what point the party of action acquired irrevocable control cannot be known. But for the Boers as a nation of horsemasters the ideal time to begin a war was as soon as the seasonal rains renewed the veldt grass—no earlier and no later. It is significant that the war did begin exactly then; and possibly, or even probably, none of the Boer proceedings after the Bloemfontein Conference had any other purpose.

Britain's Goal — A United South Africa

C. W. de KIEWIET

IN April 1897 a new High Commissioner, Sir Alfred Milner, left England for South Africa to test once again the rule of South African governorships that no man, however great, had thus far been great enough to cope with its problems. Milner did not come with instructions to force the Transvaal to come to terms. Nor was he the tool of mining magnates and financial interests. Upon the manœuvres of the Uitlanders he even looked with a hostile eye. Milner cherished the hope that the weakness of the Transvaal might yet find it out and chasten its obstinate temper. Even now it might be possible for the liberal element in the Transvaal to gain the upper hand. The President himself could not live for ever. The view that represents Milner as the agent of an imperialist Colonial Secretary, bent on breaking the Transvaal's will, does too little justice to the earnestness of Milner's search for compromise, or to the nature of British policy which was now, as always, variously moved, contradictory in its phases, and uncoordinated between its agents. In the same manner is it true that Kruger was aware of the dangers of too obdurate an attitude. Until Kruger, to the dismay of his opponents, was elected to the Presidency once more in February 1898 Milner trod warily, keeping out of sight the "big stick" of British paramountcy. No historian of feeling can read the records of these years without halting reflectively at many points where the elements of compromise approached one another, where the old President showed that the desire for understanding was alive in his heart, where even mining magnates admitted the benefits of the republican régime and sought to co-

operate with it. The anti-Boer, the anti-imperialist, and the anti-capitalist interpretations of the years before the Boer War all do insufficient justice to the complexity of events and to the character of the participants. The picture of the capitalists as men with gold in their hands, brass in their tongues, contempt in their faces, and treachery in their hearts is as untrue as the picture of an Empire robbing a petty State of its independence out of envy for its wealth, or the picture of an ignorant and perverse old man leading his State into destruction rather than yield to a modern age.

The book is yet to be written that will do full justice to the points of dispute in the last years. The Boer War was caused by two broad sets of circumstances upon which depended the numerous individual points of dispute during the last years. The first, quite clearly, was the existence of the gold-mines and the powerful financial and commercial interests whose focus was the Witwatersrand. The Jameson Raid, the Uitlander grievances, the problems of British Indians, monopolies, and tariffs were directly connected with gold-mining interests. Any attempt by the British Government to secure concessions or reforms from the Transvaal Government made it inevitably the agent of the mining magnates. By espousing the cause of the Uitlander, or by seeking to obstruct the Transvaal's use of a non-British port at Delagoa Bay, Great Britain gave its support, whether this was clearly realized in Downing Street or not, to capital and mining investments. Thus far the British policy was a good illustration of what has sometimes been called "economic imperialism." But it was by no

From C. W. de Kiewiet, *A History of South Africa, Social and Economic* (Oxford, 1941), pp. 137–139. Reprinted by permission of The Clarendon Press, Oxford.

means capitalist pressure alone that led to the violent reduction of republican independence. A second set of circumstances, more creditable than the first, and an authentic expression of British policy in South Africa and the rest of the Empire, must be placed beside the first. The Boer War was also the culmination of the British Government's lengthy quest for a united South Africa. No one who has read in detail and with care the records of British policy since the achievement of Confederation in Canada can miss the picture of a British Government groping for some means of ending South African disunity. The vision of British statesmanship was often opaque and its manœuvres were clumsy; its procedures were dilatory and its failures disconcerting. Yet since 1867 its problem had been to discern at what moment and in what manner unity might be obtained. Sir Harry Smith's annexation of the Orange River Sovereignty in 1848, Sir George Grey's plea for Confederation in 1858, and

Lord Carnarvon's clumsy annexation of the Transvaal in 1877 were failures. Each failure made a peaceful solution less possible. In the end only a great crisis could break the resistance which the events of the century had built against unity. By 1898 the question could not be avoided: could British policy any longer permit the Transvaal to speak without reprimand or act without restraint in matters that affected all South Africa vitally and closely? Where it was so clear that South Africa was naturally destined to unity, could a single community be allowed to deny that unity and to follow a course that made an unhappy separation the chief characteristic of political life? Could the Transvaal's search for alliances with foreign Powers be permitted to draw South Africa into the company of Egypt and Afghanistan, Samoa and Venezuela, each of which held the threat of an international war? The answer was finally clear. British paramountcy must prevail.

The Blunders of Imperial Diplomacy

WILLIAM L. LANGER

I<small>T</small> is as difficult to discuss the origins of the Boer War as to analyze the causes of the Crimean War. Both conflicts were slow in coming to a head and both involved a host of factors which were hopelessly intertwined. Something has already been said in a previous chapter of the complications in south Africa which followed the discovery of gold in the Transvaal and the great influx of foreigners into Johannesburg, and also of the schemes of Rhodes and his associates which eventuated in the famous Jameson raid of December 1895. This abortive attempt to overthrow the government of Kruger must be taken as the starting point of the later clash. Its importance can hardly be overestimated. By common consent of all writers it left behind it a feeling of profound suspicion and resentment. Nothing could convince the Boers after the Raid that there was not a plot afoot to take their country from them and that the British were not seeking a pretext for a fight. This feeling was enhanced by the enthusiastic reception accorded Jameson in England, by the mild treatment meted out to the raiders, and by the conduct of the parliamentary committee, which in the spring of 1897 investigated the whole affair. It was common knowledge that no serious attempt was made to get at some of the important evidence. The world generally was shocked when, after the committee had roundly castigated Rhodes, Chamberlain got up in parliament and exonerated him of dishonorable action.

The British position having been seriously compromised by Jameson's action, the government for a time seemed anxious to smooth matters over and reach some sort of adjustment of the questions at issue. Into the details we need not go. Suffice it to say that within a year the situation had again become critical. Legislation regulating immigration into the Transvaal and providing for the expulsion of undesirable foreigners created friction and caused something of a war scare in the spring of 1897. This crisis passed when Chamberlain took a strong line and the Pretoria government decided it would be best to yield. The years 1897 and 1898 were on the whole fairly quiet. The British government was deeply involved in serious imperial problems in other parts of the world, while the Transvaal generally suffered from bad times and financial difficulties.

In the meanwhile Sir Alfred Milner was sent out as high commissioner. Milner was the author of the widely acclaimed book *England in Egypt,* and was generally regarded as one of the ablest of the young imperialist group. Since the time of the Boer War he has been generally held responsible for the outbreak of the conflict. The Boers regarded him as an agent of Chamberlain and Rhodes, sent out to pick a quarrel. Not a few English writers have felt and said the same thing. We now have the illuminating papers of Milner himself, so that it is possible to form an independent judgment. From them it appears that after spending the first year in becoming acquainted with the questions at issue, the high commissioner came to the conclusion that the situation in the Transvaal offered little prospect of peaceful reform from within, and that there was no "way out of the political troubles of south Africa except reform in the Transvaal, or war."

Kruger was re-elected president for five years in February 1898 and therewith all hope of a more liberal régime evaporated. In the "scandalous" abuses of the Transvaal administration Milner saw the root of all the trouble. Looking at the question from the purely south African viewpoint, Milner wrote to Chamberlain, he, the high commissioner, would be inclined "to work up a crisis." But naturally everything would depend on the imperial outlook as a whole.

Chamberlain's reply to these revelations was detailed and unambiguous. He reminded Milner of the bases of policy agreed upon when he was sent out. They were to maintain Britain's rights under the Convention of 1884 and to avoid public pressure in regard to less important grievances. The considerations upon which these bases rested were:

(1) The conviction that a war with the Transvaal would certainly rouse antagonism in the Cape Colony, and leave behind it the most serious difficulties in the way of South African union. We felt that if a struggle was to come, it was most important that the Transvaal should be the aggressor, and that the Imperial Government should have the active sympathy of at all events a considerable section of the Dutch in the Colony. (2) We felt that the Raid has placed this country in a false position and has alienated the confidence of the Afrikander Party, and that it would be desirable that the irritation caused by this event should pass away before we resumed any pressure upon the Transvaal in regard to its internal policy. (3) We were of opinion that the waiting game was the best for this country as time must be on our side. The misgovernment in the Transvaal will in the long run produce opposition within its borders, and when the present rule of President Kruger comes to an end, as it must do before many years are over, we might confidently look for an improvement in the position. (4) A war with the Transvaal, unless upon the utmost and clearest provocation, would be extremely unpopular in this country. It would involve the despatch of a very large force and the expenditure of many millions." "Most of the grievances of which we have to complain are of a character which would not excite great sympathy in this country, and they would not be considered as sufficient to constitute a *casus belli.*" The foreign situation was a further argument against war. "We have on hand difficulties of the most serious character with France, Russia and Germany. We are engaged in an important expedition in the Sudan, and it is uncertain as yet whether the war on the north-west frontier of India has been finally concluded. We may emerge from all these troubles without a war, but I cannot conceal from myself that the prospect is more gloomy than it has ever been in my recollection. . . . Accordingly I wish to emphasize the fact that for the present at any rate our greatest interest in South Africa is peace, and that all our policy must be directed to this subject.

This exchange of letters has been quoted at length because it touches almost every aspect of the situation. The British could not go to war to bring the Transvaal into a south African federation because of danger of estranging the Dutch population at the Cape, because of the unenviable position in which the Jameson raid had placed the British government, because the grievances of the Uitlanders were not such that they would arouse much sympathy in England. Public opinion in England was opposed to war, and the government had its hands full elsewhere. Thus warned, Milner was obliged to exercise patience. The year 1898 was generally a quiet one, as things went in south Africa.

A new chapter opened with the new year. Milner paid a visit home in November and worked hard on the politicians to convince them that England must secure genuine reforms from the Transvaal government. The situation was now much more favorable, for the Germans had been bought off with the agreement regarding the Portuguese colonies, and France had received a decided setback in the Fashoda business. Kitchener had completed his work in the Sudan, and the Russians were negotiating for an agreement with respect to China. England was, for the moment, at the top of the pile and had no serious international complications to fear. But public opinion was still cool toward south Africa and the cabinet was sceptical of Milner's views. Chamberlain himself counselled caution and emphasized his desire not to hasten the crisis.

Even though Milner received little or no encouragement in London, the situation after his return to south Africa played into his hands. In the last days of December a man named Edgar, an English miner at Johannesburg, had been shot and killed by a Boer policeman. The case itself need not detain us here. The important thing is that the affair led to a marked revival of Uitlander agitation against the Kruger system and to the presentation of the first petition to Queen Victoria, which General Butler, who acted as commissioner in Milner's absence, rejected because of a technicality. In the midst of the agitation some effort was made by Kruger to reach an agreement with the mine owners. His hope was evidently that many of the outstanding questions could be removed in this way and that the bottom could thereby be knocked out of the entire opposition movement. We need not enter upon the details of the pourparlers. The British looked upon them from the outset as a mere manœuvre designed to split the ranks of the Uitlander population. When they consulted Chamberlain he discouraged them. Sir Percy Fitzpatrick has told us himself how he gave the correspondent of the London *Times* at Pretoria the money with which to bribe a Boer official in order to get the text of Kruger's proposals. The premature publication of the offer was admittedly an important reason for the breakdown of the negotiations. Whether Kruger was sincere or not it is hard to say, but it does seem that the old man had become convinced that some extension of the franchise was necessary, and that he was prepared to make concessions in this matter as fast as the opinion of his burghers would permit.

The question of the part played by the Rand capitalists in bringing about the war has always been a warmly debated one. It has been said that they were not interested in politics, and that they preferred to get along as best they could with the government rather than to start a row. Of course they were deeply involved in the conspiracy which ended in the Jameson raid, but that was an aberration. After the disaster Rhodes scrupulously kept out of the whole business. But this is certainly not the whole story. It would appear rather that the capitalists were against war so long as it was obvious that the British government would not play the game. Despite the low mining taxes in the Transvaal, they had grievances, of which the famous and obscure dynamite monopoly was the principal one, while maladministration, corruption, the liquor laws and the pass laws for laborers were others. Least talked about, however, was the most important question, that of labor supply. J. A. Hobson has shown pretty conclusively that the supply of native labor was a crucial matter on the Rand, and that in June 1899 there was a shortage of 12,000 men. He has shown further, on the basis of remarks made by the capitalists themselves, that they hoped, if they got control of the Transvaal government, to make a saving of two and a half million pounds sterling annually by securing for themselves an unrestricted labor supply and thus lowering the wage-rate.

Now it is worth noting that the capitalists, who, according to Fitzpatrick, did not want to introduce the question of the franchise into the negotiations for the "Great Deal," did ask that the government assist the mines in getting labor, that it enforce the liquor laws, and that it admit to the executive council an "independent" financier like Rothschild to control future taxation. When the whole project fell flat through the unwillingness of the government to accept these terms, the financial interests began to take the lead in the great campaign of villification that followed. Rhodes may have stayed in the background, but the fact remains that he controlled the Johannesburg *Star* and the Transvaal *Leader,* the *Cape Times* and other south African newspapers, to say nothing of some of the London dailies. His friend Harmsworth's *Daily Mail* was one of the most violent enemies of the Boers; the Liberal *Daily News* was acquired by his friends and pressed into service; the London *Times* championed the Uitlanders and demanded a forward policy, for reasons that are not clear. Furthermore, in April 1899 Rhodes became president of the powerful South African League, representing the British nationalists as against the Dutch Afrikaner Bond. The Outlanders' Council, founded in June 1899 at Johannesburg, was patently under the direction of the capitalists, who at this time healed the split in their own ranks which had occurred after the Jameson raid and who thenceforth pulled together.

In April 1899 the Uitlanders sent to the Queen a petition recounting their grievances. There were more than 21,000 signatures attached, which according to Milner were on the whole genuine and according to the Boers largely forged. Milner followed up the petition with the famous "helot" despatch of May 4, in which he reviewed the hardships of the Uitlanders, and declared that "the true remedy is to strike at the root of all these injuries, the political impotence of the injured. What diplomatic protests will never accomplish, a fair measure of Uitlander representation would gradually but surely bring about. . . . The case for intervention is overwhelming." Then, to drive the point home, he issued a significant warning:

The spectacle of thousands of British subjects kept permanently in the position of helots, constantly chafing under undoubted grievances, and calling vainly to Her Majesty's Government for redress, does steadily undermine the influence and reputation of Great Britain and the respect for the British Government within its own dominions. A certain section of the press, and not in the Transvaal only, preaches openly and constantly the doctrine of a Republic embracing all South Africa, and supports it by menacing references to the armaments of the Transvaal, its alliance

with the Orange Free State, and the active sympathy which in case of war it would receive from a section of Her Majesty's subjects. I regret to say that this doctrine, supported as it is by a ceaseless stream of malignant lies about the intentions of the British Government, is producing a great effect upon a large number of our Dutch fellow-colonists. . . . I can see nothing which will put a stop to this mischievous propaganda but some striking proof of the intention, if it is the intention, of Her Majesty's Government not to be ousted from its position in South Africa.

Before leaving this despatch a few words of comment will be in order. In the first place, it ought to be pointed out that there has always been much difference of opinion as to the extent of the grievances of the Uitlanders. It is impossible at this date to make any definite pronouncement, but the conscientious reader will want to consult the writings of men like Stead and Hobson before accepting in full the statements of Fitzpatrick and E. T. Cook, to say nothing of less responsible imperialists. Hobson was in the Transvaal in the summer and autumn of 1899 and declared that he could secure little concrete evidence of oppression, though the place was full of stock stories that could not be corroborated. "The notion that Englishmen or White British subjects have commonly been made the victims of oppression and terrorism is grotesquely and utterly false," he said. "So far as practical freedom of action, speech and publication are concerned, there was no place upon the continent of Europe which could for a moment compare with it (Johannesburg)." "There are liars and credulous folk in every land; but for a minute detailed mendacity and the wanton acceptance of the same, South Africa stands pre-eminent." There was, of course, corruption and maladministration, but corruption had been more or less fostered by the financial interests themselves, and if it had been as bad as it was made out to be, it might have been reasonably urged that the capitalists "would have found it cheaper and safer to buy the Boer Government than to enter a troublesome political campaign for its reformation or its overthrow."

Hobson was convinced that reform would have come in the course of time and through the pressure of circumstances, and Professor Walker, in his *History of South Africa,* has shown that there was more than a merely negligible measure of reform between 1896 and 1899. Furthermore, by Milner's own admission only a percentage of the foreigners in Johannesburg desired the franchise. Most of them were transients, who had no desire to give up their citizenship, but were interested chiefly in making their pile and then clearing out. Finally, a word about the much-discussed Dutch conspiracy to oust the British from south Africa. Talk of this plot became prevalent in South African circles after the victory of the Afrikander Bond in the Cape elections of the autumn of 1898. In actual fact there was little justification for the imputation of disloyalty so far as the Cape Dutch were concerned. The Bond and its leader, Hofmeyr, had always been for the connexion with Britain and in 1899 did their utmost to effect a peaceful settlement. They had no use for Krugerism and certainly had no desire to spread that system to the whole of south Africa. That there were some hotheaded young bloods in the Transvaal there can be no doubt, but there is little evidence to support the idea of a general policy aimed at ejecting the British. In fact the idea is rather preposterous. "Of all the disreputable, contemptible and discreditable proceedings by which a nation has ever been jockeyed into war," wrote W. T. Stead, "this fighting for the paramountcy is about the worst." His opinion was echoed by an anonymous writer in the *Edinburgh Review,* who declared that "the notion that there is a formidable Dutch conspiracy 'to oust British influence . . . from South Africa' is the strangest nightmare that ever afflicted the most nervous of 'Imperialist' minds."

The simple truth of the matter is that the franchise demand and the spectre of the Dutch conspiracy cannot be examined on their merits. Milner had come to the conclusion that the franchise would do better as a lever than a host of lesser questions which concerned the capitalists rather than the Uitlanders as a whole. The conspiracy alarm, too, was probably meant chiefly as an incentive to British public opinion. Milner was working for a crisis, though it should be carefully noted that this is not saying that he wanted war. He was ready for armed conflict if it proved unavoidable, but he undoubtedly hoped to get what he wanted by mere pressure. Rhodes told a British cabinet minister in the spring of 1899 that Kruger was "only bluffing." "If you were to employ your troops you could undoubtedly bring him to subjection." To his friend Beit he wrote: "Nothing will make Kruger fire a shot." These same ideas recur in the Milner correspondence. Here are a few excerpts from his letters at the time: May 17, 1899: "I don't want war, but I admit I begin to think it may be the only way out." "Absolute downright determination plus a large temporary increase of force will assure a climb down. It is 20 to 1." May 24, 1899: "My view has been and still is, in spite of all these alarms and excursions, that if we are perfectly determined we shall win without a fight or with a mere apology for one."

The great obstacle to the realization of Milner's policy was the negative attitude of British opinion and the resulting unwillingness of the cabinet to embark upon a policy that might lead to war. Milner's helot despatch was written with the idea that it should be published and that it would serve as an effective irritant. But for the time being it had to be held back and Milner was obliged to accept the mediation of President Steyn of the Orange Free State, who arranged a meeting with Kruger at Bloemfontein. There discussions took place between May 30 and June 5. From the outset they were doomed to failure. Milner had been instructed by Chamberlain to show a conciliatory spirit, but instead of doing so "he bombarded the president with dialectical artillery, bowling over in summary fashion his arguments, making debating scores off him, and eventually driving the old man to an attitude of obstinate despair." It was certainly a mistake to try to deal with the old Vortrekker as though he were a polished European diplomat, but it was positively fatal to the Conference to do what Milner did, namely to demand a straight five-year retrospective franchise in place of the existing fourteen-year franchise, and to refuse to discuss other matters until this demand was accepted. Kruger seems to have come with the idea that all the "nasty questions" were to be discussed. Naturally he was not prepared to accept a measure which, he felt, would deliver his country into the hands of the Uitlanders, without some sort of guarantee of a *quid pro quo*. Even then it was Milner who broke off the conference, too hastily, as he himself acknowledged later.

Chamberlain was alarmed by Milner's uncomprising attitude and was not at all certain that Kruger had said his last word. It was essential, he wired Milner, that the Pretoria government be put clearly in the wrong. But the mistake had been made and in the succeeding weeks the colonial secretary gradually turned up the road marked out by Milner. He published the famous helot despatch and his own reply adopting the case of the Uitlanders. The despatch, says Walker, "clanged like a trumpet-call presaging war." Perhaps for this very reason it did not go over with the public nearly as well as had been hoped. Chamberlain attempted to secure the support of the Liberals for a forward policy. He told Campbell-Bannerman that he was, and always had been, striving for a peaceful settlement, "but he was afraid that a demonstration . . . would be necessary. It would, however, be a game of bluff, and it was impossible to play that game if the Opposition did not support the Government." But the Liberals were unwilling to support an "open military demonstration." Furthermore, the cabinet, convinced that a war would be very unpopular, refused to commit itself to anything beyond firm language and protests.

While the British government was marking time, all sorts of pressure was being brought to bear on Kruger by the Dutch leaders at the Cape. The Dutch and German governments too sent strong advice to yield. Such a course was not easy, for the burghers were filled with distrust. They hated that *verdomde Kimberlain,* who, they felt convinced, had been bought by Rhodes with a generous block of Consolidated Goldfields stock. Even reputed progressives, like Joubert, were opposed to concessions, and it was widely believed that the British were merely bluffing — that they would not fight. Nevertheless, Kruger had offered a seven-year franchise during the Bloemfontein discussions, and on July 18 he got the Volksraad to accept such a scheme. Chamberlain was elated by this turn of events. He inspired a statement in the *Times* saying that the crisis was at an end, and he wired to Milner: "If . . . President South African Republic has really given seven years retroactive franchise and five seats (in the Volksraad to the Rand), I congratulate you on great victory. No one would dream of fighting over two years in qualification period and President South African Republic will have been driven by successive steps to almost exact position taken by you. We ought to make most of this and accept it as basis of settlement."

Milner was horrified. The *Times* article, he telegraphed Chamberlain, had "created consternation among British party" in south Africa. The Transvaal offer, he declared, was far from satisfactory. At the same time the south African press and the Uitlanders raised a howl and reiterated their demand for the five-year franchise as a minimum. All this fuss made Chamberlain waver. He had, so his biographer points out, intended from the beginning to secure guarantees for the satisfactory working of the proposed franchise scheme, and secured cabinet approval for his next step. On July 27 he proposed a joint inquiry into the working of the new law. This idea was particularly distasteful to the Boers, who regarded it as interference in their domestic affairs. They therefore accepted the suggestion of President Steyn and, after consultation with the British agent at Pretoria, put forward (August 19) a five-year-franchise plan with the assignment of at least a quarter of the seats in the Rand to the mining areas, but all this on condition that the Imperial government drop the claim to suzerainty, interfere no more in the internal affairs of the Republic, and agree to refer minor points in dispute to arbitration.

No doubt something might have been done with this offer, if the British negotiators had been willing to make the most of it. The press of south Africa, controlled by the capitalists, was demanding nothing less than the whole hog, and Milner was constantly insisting that all that was needed was firmness: "There is at bottom a very great indisposition to fight on the part of the Boers, not only in the Colony and Orange Free State, but even in the Transvaal itself. . . . The larger our force, the smaller is likely to be theirs, and I think one good slap in the face may dissipate them" (August 2, 1899); "They will collapse if we don't weaken, or rather if we go on steadily turning the screw" (August 16, 1899). With such assurances dinning in his ears Chamberlain was bound to take a cynical attitude toward the Boer offers. In a resounding speech at Highbury on August 26 he declared: "Mr. Kruger dribbles out reforms like water from a squeezed sponge, and he either accompanies his offers with conditions which he knows to be impossible, or he refuses to allow us to make a satisfactory investigation of the nature of these reforms. . . . The sands are running down in the glass. . . . The knot must be loosened . . . or else we shall have to find other ways of untying it."

A few days later the colonial secretary sent a despatch accepting the Boer proposals without the provisos, on the plea that the British government could not abandon its rights under the conventions or give up the substance of suzerainty. Chamberlain later maintained that this despatch was one of "qualified acceptance" and that he had agreed to nine tenths of the Boer proposals. This is absurd. The Chamberlain reply was what the Boers thought it was — a rejection of the terms offered. They therefore withdrew the offer of the five-year franchise and fell back on the earlier British suggestion of a joint inquiry into the working of the seven-year franchise. It had been explicitly stated that the proposal of a five-year franchise did not involve a rejection of the joint inquiry on the part of the Boers, but Chamberlain now refused to entertain his own earlier suggestion. He had evidently fixed on a line of action and had no intention of swerving. In a letter to Milner (September 2) he stated that he had asked for a cabinet to consider the terms of an ultimatum. The situation, he pointed out, was a difficult one, for "the technical *casus belli* is a very weak one and, thanks to past concessions and weaknesses, our hands are tied in regard to many matters which might otherwise be put forward to justify extreme action." Neither the Uitlanders nor the British at the Cape, he continued, were wholly without reproach, for the former were

unfortunately identified with money-making — with the Raid — and are not supposed to be capable of much self-sacrifice even for a holy cause — and the latter are quite too ready to take all the profits of a war in the shape of Imperial expenditure while doing nothing themselves but shouting on every occasion that they will cut the painter if the Imperial Government does not do everything they want and do it as quickly as they consider possible and desirable.

There were other obstacles to a forward policy. Chamberlain confessed himself surprised that so much progress had been made:

It is a great thing to say that the majority of the people have, as I believe, recognised that there is a greater issue than the franchise or the grievances of the Uitlanders at stake, and that our supremacy in South Africa and our existence as a great Power in the world are

involved in the result of our present controversy. Three months ago we could not — that
is, we should not have been allowed to — go
to war on this issue. Now — although still
most unwillingly and with a large minority
against us, we shall be sufficiently supported."
But "we must play out this game *selon les
règles* and it seems to me to-day that we ought
to exhaust the franchise proposals and get a
clear refusal before . . . we ask for more. If
and when we ask for more it means war, and
therefore, before we do this, we must have a
sufficient force in South Africa to defend ourselves during the time that will be required to
get a full fighting force into the country. . . .

This letter would seem to indicate that
by the beginning of September negotiation
was simply a blind so far as Chamberlain
was concerned. He had convinced himself
that British opinion was sufficiently persuaded to make it possible to go on, but
the whole situation was such that more
time was needed to get troops to the scene.
In order to gain time the franchise issue
was to be wrung dry, but Kruger was not
to escape even if he gave in, for in that
event the British, like the French in 1870,
would bring forward more demands, knowing full well that when they asked for more
it would mean war. With this program
Chamberlain went before the cabinet and
carried his colleagues with him. It was decided to send 10,000 more men to south
Africa and in the meanwhile to string out
the discussions with Pretoria. In a despatch
of the same date Chamberlain insisted on
the five-year franchise without conditions
and, failing that, reserved to the British
government the right "to consider the situation *de novo*, and to formulate their own
proposals for a final settlement."

There was, by this time, no turning back,
for the government was committed. Salisbury, Balfour and other members of the
cabinet gave in to the colonial secretary,
but only reluctantly and with misgivings.
The prime minister wrote to Lansdowne on
August 30 that Milner's view was "too
heated, if you consider the intrinsic significance and importance of the things which

are in controversy." But, he went on, "it
recks little to think of that now. What he
has done cannot be effaced. We have to
act upon a moral field prepared for us by
him and his jingo supporters. And therefore I see before us the necessity for considerable military effort — and all for people whom we despise and for territory
which will bring no profit and no power to
England." Almost to the very end Salisbury seems to have hoped that Milner
would prove right in his contention that
the Boers would back down before a show
of force.

But there was absolutely no chance of
that. In south Africa the exodus of the
Uitlanders from Johannesburg had already
begun. The local press was full of atrocity
stories which were assiduously copied in
the English press. Popular excitement was
rising high and matters had already been
pushed to the very verge of war. Kruger
rejected Chamberlain's proposal on September 17 and the cabinet had to decide on
the next step. Salisbury favored a temporiz-
ing policy until the time when reinforcements should have reached the scene, but
Chamberlain carried the cabinet with his
suggestion for secret mobilization. On September 22 he wired triumphantly to Milner: "Cabinet unanimous and resolves to
see matter through." Another despatch was
to be sent by steamer so as to gain another
four weeks for preparation.

By this time even Salisbury seems to
have become convinced, or, shall we say,
seems to have convinced himself that more
than Uitlander grievances were at issue and
that there was a Dutch conspiracy to drive
the British out of south Africa. It may be
that the publication of Fitzpatrick's *The
Transvaal from Within* had something to
do with his conversion. Fitzpatrick was one
of the capitalist group who had taken an
active part in the revolutionary movement
which eventuated in the Jameson raid. He
had, in general, served as liaison officer between the mining interests and the Uitlander agitators. His book, while still in
manuscript, had been read by Milner late

in 1898, and is said to have confirmed him in the policy which led to war. It is said that the book made a deep impression also upon Salisbury when it was published in England in September 1899. At any rate the prime minister seems to have swallowed the plot-story whole. He wrote to the Queen on September 23: "It is impossible to avoid believing that the Boers really aim at setting up a South African Republic, consisting of the Transvaal, the Orange Free State and Your Majesty's Colony. It is impossible to account in any other manner for their rejection of our most moderate proposals." And on October 5 he declared in a letter to Lord Courtney that while he could not convict Kruger of conspiracy in a court of law, he had become convinced, from watching the course of negotiations "that Kruger was using the oppression of the Outlanders as a lever to exact from England a renunciation of suzerainty; and the conduct of President Steyn and Mr. Schreiner (prime minister at the Cape), of the Africanders generally and of their sympathisers in Europe, has brought home to me the belief that there is an understanding among the leaders of Dutch opinion, and their aspiration is the restoration of South Africa to the Dutch race."

The British were now rushing troops to south Africa and were merely sparring for time in the hope of getting 70,000 men to the scene before the storm broke. Recognizing the futility of further discussion the Transvaal government, after asking for the British terms and being put off, drew up an ultimatum demanding that the troops be withdrawn from the frontiers, that all reinforcements sent out since June 1 be recalled within a reasonable period, and that the forces then on the sea should not be landed at any south African port. This ultimatum was presented on October 9, and simply forestalled a British one. The British government simply declared these "peremptory demands" impossible of discussion and therewith the war began.

It is hardly necessary to say much by way of recapitulation. No one would deny

that the south African situation had for years been a most difficult one, complicated as it was by the peculiar race problem and by the troubles that were bound to arise from the establishment of great mining interests and the influx of thousands of foreigners into an essentially backward agrarian state. Things had really come to a head with the Jameson raid, which had set all these antagonisms in a lurid light and had left an atmosphere of distrust in which it was nearly impossible to negotiate in any cordial way. Both the capitalists and the workers in the Transvaal had undoubted grievances, though they were probably not as serious as Fitzpatrick, for example, made them out to be. It seems unlikely that the Transvaal government could have maintained its exclusive policy for very much longer in the face of changing conditions. At any rate it was not given the chance. Rhodes and the other capitalists were set upon a federation of south Africa and that implied control of the Transvaal government. Having failed to get what they wanted from Kruger they made use of the Uitlander grievances, mobilized the press which they controlled and raised the hue and cry of the Dutch conspiracy. Milner's views suited them perfectly and those views were that England must intervene in the domestic affairs of the Transvaal, which she was hardly justified in doing, no matter what opinion one may hold of the unhappy suzerainty issue. Milner finally convinced Chamberlain, who was at first hopeful and circumspect but came round after the Fashoda crisis. He wrote to the Queen retrospectively that he had "long felt that the differences between this country and the Transvaal could only be settled by force."

Affairs might well have been brought to a head in the spring of 1898 excepting for the fact that British public opinion was so little interested in Uitlander grievances and the government was so deeply involved in serious questions of international politics that it was absolutely unwilling to follow Milner and Chamberlain. It was not until

Germany had been squared by the agreement on the Portuguese colonies and France had been take care of in the Fashoda crisis that the field became clear. Even then it required a long campaign of propaganda to bring the British public into line, and to convert Lord Salisbury, who disliked both capitalists and jingoes. In the meanwhile negotiations dragged on, marked throughout by a certain insincerity. The British consistently refused to submit their final terms and thereby gave the Transvaalers good reason to suppose that every concession would be followed by further demands and that the root of the whole business was the desire of the British to get control of the Transvaal and its great wealth. Whether Milner actually believed that the Boers would not fight it is hard to say. In any event his policy of bluff was a dangerous one, which, as he himself recognized, might lead to war. But he did not fear war. In his opinion only "an apology for a fight" would be necessary. A "slap in the face" would do the business. Had he appreciated the seriousness of the struggle on which England was embarked so lightheartedly, he would undoubtedly have made greater efforts to find another way out. Chamberlain showed himself throughout to be much better informed and statesmanlike and came only gradually to the conclusion that force was the only method that would bring a solution. Salisbury and other cabinet ministers, as we have seen, were even more sceptical and reluctant. They allowed Milner to push them into a crisis from which there was no decent escape except through war.

South Africa: Another Canada
or Another United States?

RONALD ROBINSON, JOHN GALLAGHER, AND
ALICE DENNY

THE crisis of March and April 1896 persuaded Chamberlain and Selborne that the imperial supremacy of influence had collapsed. Unless it could be restored quickly, and the South African states soon formed into a British dominion, the superior wealth and power of the Transvaal seemed likely to draw the colonies out of the empire into a "United States of South Africa." The Prime Minister was sceptical of this cataclysmic view. On 30 March, 1896, he read a Colonial Office memorandum about imperial prospects in south Africa. Drafted by Selborne, so important a document must have been discussed with Chamberlain before it was sent. It is perhaps the best evidence of the fundamental considerations which inspired Chamberlain and Selborne henceforward and which in the end dragged the ministry into the Boer War.

British African Dominion, question of creating.
Are the British Possessions in South Africa more likely to become separated from the British Empire,
1. If they become confederated with the two Republics under the British flag as a British African Dominion, or
2. If they remain as now separate units under various forms of Government and continue to have as their neighbours two independent Republics?
  In endeavouring to answer this question I take as my postulate the fact, as I believe it to be, that the key to the future of South Africa is in the Transvaal. It is the richest spot on earth. The only properly speaking populous spots in South Africa are already within it; and while the population of Cape Colony, of Natal, of Rhodesia etc. will increase but slowly and gradually, the population of the Transvaal has increased, and will continue to increase, by leaps and bounds, and in fifty years time will probably be reckoned in millions.
  My postulate therefore is that the Transvaal is going to be by far the richest, by far the most populous part of South Africa, that it is going to be the natural capital state and centre of South African commercial, social and political life. . . .
  . . . The Transvaal will be the market for South Africa: the market for the manufactures of Cape Colony and Natal: the market for the agricultural products of those Colonies and of Rhodesia. The commercial interest of the closest connexion with the Transvaal will outweigh all other considerations. These British Colonies will sue for closer commercial union. The Transvaal will reply that so long as these Colonies remain British they will not grant it; that they have no intention of becoming British, but that if these Colonies will unite with them in forming a United Republic of South Africa they will welcome them with open arms.
  If the Transvaal were always going to remain a Dutch Republic, I admit that this danger would not be so imminent. Racial jealousies might temporarily postpone the effects of commercial interests. But . . . the Transvaal cannot permanently remain a Dutch Republic. There has never been a census; but the best information obtainable gives a maxi-

From Ronald Robinson and John Gallagher, with Alice Denny, *Africa and the Victorians: The Official Mind of Imperialism* (London, 1961), pp. 434; 436–441; 444–457. Reprinted by permission of Macmillan & Co., Ltd.

mum of 25,000 male Boers and a minimum of 50,000 Uitlanders, of whom ¾ are British. Before Jameson's criminal blunder the Uitlanders were said to be pouring into Transvaal at the rate of 500 males a week. Just think what would be the result of 10 or 20 years of an immigration maintained at one-fifth or even one-tenth of this rate! Therefore according to all the experience of history, this country so powerful in its future wealth and population . . . situated at the geographical centre of political South Africa would assuredly attract to itself all British Colonies in South Africa.

A great part in the working out of this problem will be played by the Delagoa Bay Railway. If we could secure the control over it we should effect two great results. We should, by holding the balance even between the South African railway systems give an immense assistance to the Cape Colony, to Natal, and to the Orange Free State to maintain their commercial and financial position against the Transvaal. We should also bring conviction at last to the Transvaal Government that their best interests lay in coming to a complete understanding with us. They would feel themselves irrevocably hemmed in. They would renounce their foreign intrigues as of no further practical utility, and they would come to terms with us. If on the other hand the control of the railway passed to the Transvaal, or to a Foreign Power working with the Transvaal against British interests, the results would be very serious. They could then secure a monopoly of all Transvaal trade for the Delagoa Bay Railway with the effect not only of supplanting British imports by (say) German imports, and not only of inflicting grievous commercial injury on the trading classes of the Cape Colony and Natal, but they could also reduce the Governments of those two Colonies and that of the Orange Free State to the verge of financial bankruptcy, so dependent are they upon their railway revenue. It needs no words to prove what a powerful use could be made of this instrument in squeezing the British South African Colonies into joining in a United South African Republic. . . .

My opinion, therefore, is that

1. If we can succeed in uniting all South Africa into a Confederacy on the model of the Dominion of Canada and under the British Flag, the probability is that that confeder-

acy will not become a United States of South Africa.

2. If South Africa remains as now a congeries of separate States, partly British Colonies and partly Republics, it will inevitably amalgamate itself into a United States of South Africa.

3. That we must secure the control of the Delagoa Bay Railway for the British Imperial Government if Portugal is not able to retain the control herself.

The Prime Minister unfortunately did not record his comments on the colonial ministers' argument. They doubtless exaggerated to make a case. But according to the canons of supremacy which had held good since mid-Victorian times, their logic had force. That the south African reaction to the Raid, together with the economic revolution, had done immense damage to the old imperial paramountcy of influence could not be denied. Paramountcy since the Eighteen sixties had meant two things: the exclusion of rival European states; and power enough to guide South African development toward a loyal imperial confederation. For nearly forty years British ministers thought they had been building their dominion upon the rock of Cape Colony, and more recently, upon the Cape Colony and Rhodesia. By 1896 they knew that they had built on sand. The real stone of South African union lay out of reach in the Transvaal. . . .

In appraising the fall of paramountcy, Chamberlain and Selborne were contending that the imperial government itself must now intervene directly, if South Africa was to be welded into a British dominion. Since the end of the Eighteen eighties, Chamberlain's ambition had been to reassert the "Imperial factor." Many of his colleagues apparently wondered if it was not too late already. The memorandum of 1896 seems to have been addressed to Salisbury and other ministers who, like Ripon in 1894, doubted whether the Transvaal should be forced into an imperial dominion, or indeed whether a South African confederation would best secure British influence or stay for long within the empire. To most Liberals and some conservatives "supremacy" over white dominions seemed by now a word to call fools into a circle. Hence the Prime Minister is likely to have argued against Chamberlain and Selborne in the crisis of 1896 that it might be better for British interests to be content with a divided South Africa than to try and force the incorporation of the Transvaal. It hardly seemed worth while to risk a Boer war in pursuit of a South African dominion, when imperial authority over dominions was becoming a fiction. The colonial ministers' memorandum of March was meant to rebutt that objection. They asserted that unless the Transvaal could be controlled once more from Delagoa Bay, or be swiftly incorporated into a dominion, South Africa would be united as a republic. They hinted that British trade and investment would be damaged by this outcome. Perhaps they argued in the Cabinet Defence Committee that a United States of South Africa would deprive Britain of the Cape Town naval base.

It seemed in 1896 to be still vital to imperial security. Goschen at the Admiralty gave warning that the Navy could not keep the Mediterranean route to the East open for merchant ships in case of war. Much shipping would be diverted round the Cape and to cope with it, the Admiralty was already extending coaling facilities and docks at the Cape and Mauritius.

Strategy was one element in the Colonial Office pressure for an active South African policy. But there were wider considerations as well. In proclaiming the bankruptcy of the traditional system of influence, the memorandum implied the necessity of a new departure. Chamberlain and Selborne insisted that it was worth the effort and the risk. Their older Tory colleagues doubted it. At bottom, the difference in outlook on the South African crisis reflected two different predictions about the future of the empire as a whole. Chamberlain hoped to reconstruct it as a unit of

defence, and perhaps also of trade, under a central federal authority in London. Without imperial federation, he doubted whether the United Kingdom would survive as a great power in the twentieth century alongside the continental giants, the United States and Russia. If South Africa was to be included in a federation of the whole empire, it was urgent to absorb the Transvaal and make a British South African union before it became too late. Salisbury and the Conservative leaders on the other hand were more impressed with the hazards than the needs for haste. They had had more experience of the immense obstacles in the way of imperial federation. They doubted whether the growth of Canada and Australia towards independent nationhood could be compressed into a federated empire. More sceptical about the possibility of strengthening central authority over dominions in matters of defence, foreign affairs and trade, they were in no hurry to turn South Africa into another dominion. In this sense perhaps, the memorandum of March 1896 was the new imperial federationists' manifesto in the South African case.

But upon the need to restore supremacy over South Africa the Colonial ministers and their critical colleagues all agreed. If they were divided about the degree of risk to be taken, the Cabinet accepted the breakdown of indirect influence and colonial agency as a fact. Ministers resigned themselves to intervention. At the same time they did not want another Anglo-Boer war. The Prime Minister and the rest of the Cabinet thought Chamberlain "impulsive." But it seemed that only two ways of strengthening imperial influence remained; to press Kruger with the full weight of British diplomacy into enfranchising the *Uitlanders*; and to get control of Delagoa Bay. Of the two, Chamberlain and Selborne regarded Delagoa Bay as much the more effective issue. It was there that German interference might be blocked, the British grip on the Transvaal regained and the South African balance redressed in favour of the colonies. *Uitlander* representation and a British confederation would surely follow. On the other hand, to enfranchise the immigrants would not in itself solve the question. Chamberlain and Selborne knew that it would only lead to a British republic. Their task was as much to bring the unwilling *Uitlanders* as the intransigent Boers into the empire.

During the remainder of 1896, Salisbury, urged on by Chamberlain, pursued the main chance in Lisbon. The Prime Minister's pessimism about extracting Delagoa Bay or the railway from Portugal was confirmed. German and French opposition strengthened Portugal's natural reluctance to part with her possession. In December the Colonial Secretary complained: "Delagoa Bay is the key of the situation in S[outh] Africa — it is to us of supreme importance; yet we can get no kind of satisfaction [from Lisbon]." He pressed Salisbury "to take a more decided line." "Could we make [the Portuguese Government] choose between us and Germany?" The Prime Minister with all his diplomatic troubles over China and the Sudan, decided that nothing could be done to compel Portugal; and Chamberlain bowed to his authority. In Lisbon as at Pretoria the Colonial Secretary concluded: ". . . we have nothing to do but to stand upon our rights and wait events. . . ."

For the next eighteen months Chamberlain and his colleagues watched and waited. They reverted to the policy of patience. There were good reasons. Ministers believed that the public's enthusiasm for empire was by no means ripe for war with the Transvaal — evidence enough that they were not driven on by imperialist hysteria in the Country. As Chamberlain told the new High Commissioner, Sir Alfred Milner, unless the Boers were the aggressor, a war would be "extremely unpopular" in Britain. And it would "certainly rouse antagonism in the Cape Colony, and leave behind it the most serious difficulties in the way of South African union." Hicks Beach was protesting against the bills he would

have to meet for expeditions in the Sudan and in west Africa, fighting in India and the troubles in Crete and China. "You and I," he complained to the Prime Minister, "can remember what happened in 1878–80. Our Afghan and Zulu misfortunes were the main cause of our defeat [at the election] in 1880. We tried a forward policy in too many places at once. I am afraid of the same thing now. . . . Chamberlain will try to do a good deal if you don't stop him." The older ministers were still frightened of the shadow of Midlothian. They still remembered vividly the disasters which Carnarvon's annexation of the Transvaal had brought down both upon the government at Home and upon the empire in South Africa. And the expected collision with France over Fashoda dictated caution in dealing with Germany, with Portugal and with Kruger. Chamberlain, himself, now accepted that:

. . . Our policy for the present was to let the Boers "stew in their own juice", fight out their internal quarrels and not be able to raise prejudice and confuse the issues by pointing to external interference as the danger to be feared.

The decision may be right or wrong, but I intend that it shall have a fair trial. . . .

DELAGOA BAY: THE LAST CHANCE, 1898

Negotiations had opened and closed in Lisbon, but Salisbury refused to go to extremes for the purpose. He had a certain regard for international legality, a sharp sense of the borderline where diplomacy lurched over the brink of war. The Prime Minister had done no more than offer bankrupt Portugal a loan to be secured upon the revenues of Mozambique and her other African colonies.

In June 1898 the Germans threatened to work against Britain everywhere, unless Salisbury admitted them to a share in the loan — and in the Portuguese colonies in case of default. The clash with France in the Sudan was near, and Salisbury felt it wiser to settle with Berlin. The basis of his proposal was that if Portugal accepted loans from Britain and Germany, the customs revenue of Mozambique south of the Zambesi, and Angola north of Egibo, would be pledged to the British. The remainder of the two Portuguese colonies would stand security for the Germans. But Bulow, trying to raise the price of German abstention in the Transvaal and at Delagoa Bay, asked in addition for Blantyre, Timor, Walfisch Bay.

Chamberlain in August was dissatisfied not only with German demands but with Salisbury's weakness. The Colonial Secretary wanted Delagoa Bay immediately. It was not enough to hope that Lisbon would accept a loan and then to wait for her default. Salisbury's proposals left the supreme objective dependent on too many contingencies. But the Prime Minister, on holiday in France, replied that it was impracticable to do more:

I do not see how any different arrangement, giving us control of Lorenzo (sic) Marques before default, is possible. It is only after default that Portugal would have any motive whatever for conceding to us control over Lorenzo (sic) Marques or any other portions of her Colonies. Default is the essence of the whole matter. Occupant Portugal would have no reason to surrender any right or any territory.

If you think this was not what the Cabinet understood by the proposals, further negotiation had better be deferred till they meet again. There is in reality no hurry as Portugal is resolved at present to borrow from nobody.

Salisbury apparently had some respect for the rights of the occupant in a territorial question. Nor had he much hope that Portugal would accept a loan on the Anglo-German terms. It seemed to him now as for ten years past, that there was but a hollow chance of getting effective control over Delagoa Bay and its railway. At this Chamberlain seems to have lost faith in the Anglo-German arrangement. On 19 August he wrote to Balfour: ". . . the only advantage to us is the promise of Germany's abstention from further interference in Delagoa Bay and the Transvaal — in other

words, we pay blackmail to Germany to induce her not to interfere. . . ." But to stave off German meddling in South Africa would not restore imperial supremacy over the Transvaal republic. Four days later Chamberlain wrote: ". . . I am much less eager than I was for any arrangement, and I should not break my heart if the negotiations [with Germany] came to an end. I never anticipated that the Germans would be so greedy."

Salisbury and Balfour however went on to sign the Anglo-German agreement. It was too late to break off negotiations without giving offence in Berlin. The treaty, it was true, was no guarantee that Portugal would accept Anglo-German loans or that she would default on repayment; and until she did, the clauses assigning practical control of Delagoa Bay to Britain would not come into force. But the agreement had its advantages. As Balfour put it:

. . . it secures for us the absolute exclusion of every other Power, including Germany, from what, for shortness, I may call our sphere of influence — in other words, Germany resigns . . . a claim to regard Delagoa Bay as a port of international interest, whose fate Portugal and England could not be permitted to settle at their own sweet will. Resigning this, she also resigns all concern in Transvaal matters. That she would ever have actively supported the Transvaal is, indeed, more than doubtful; but unquestionably her supposed friendliness to the Boers encouraged them to adopt a policy towards this country, which, now that they are shut out from all hope of European assistance, may perhaps be modified to our advantage.

We obtain further a complete defensive alliance with Germany against any third Power desiring to intervene in Mozambique or Angola.

The Anglo-German treaty isolated the Transvaal from European aid. It ended the efforts which Germany had made since 1894 to claim compensation for any change in the international status of Mozambique and the Transvaal. But as German interference had never been a serious menace to imperial supremacy in South Africa, so the removing of it did little to restore that supremacy. The rise of the Transvaal and the internal conflicts within South Africa, not the rivalry within the European balance, had done most to slacken the British hold upon South Africa. By 23 October the Portuguese government had rejected Anglo-German financial aid and raised a loan in Paris instead. Salisbury's gloomy forecast had been fulfilled. Delagoa Bay, the "trump card in the game of uniting S[outh] Africa as a British state" had once again eluded Chamberlain and Milner.

By the end of 1898, all the British moves to restore paramountcy and to counteract the political and commercial preponderance of the Transvaal had failed. The Portuguese would not part with Delagoa Bay. Hope of a northern Rand in Rhodesia had faded. Every attempt to breach the burghers' monopoly of power in the Transvaal on behalf of the *Uitlanders* had boomeranged; and the nationalist reaction had turned towards Kruger the sympathies of the Orange Free State and many of the Cape Dutch. In spite of Rhodes' re-entry into politics and his organisation of the South Africa League, the Bondsmen won the Cape election in the autumn of 1898 and took office under Schreiner. The best that Milner expected of such a ministry was neutrality; whereas at the Transvaal election of February, Kruger had won an overwhelming majority. The *Uitlanders'* hope of victory for the liberal burghers had again been disappointed.

THE RESTORATION OF SUPREMACY

It seemed to Milner that only one way to restore supremacy was left — the British government must compel Kruger to admit the *Uitlanders* to power. As early as February 1898 his mind was turning toward this desperate solution. "Looking at the question from a purely South African point of view," he had written, "I should be inclined to work up to a crisis. . . ." Chamberlain however had damped his heat. After an interview with the Colonial Secretary, one of Milner's officials reported in July:

. . . Chamberlain will *not* do anything, owing to the fear that the party would suffer by proposing a line of policy which would not command the support of the Opposition, or even of a certain number of the supporters of the Govt. . . . [Chamberlain] insisted on the fact that public opinion would not support him in taking action unless a distinct and serious breach of the Convention could be brought home [against the Transvaal]. . . .

A war to free the Johannesburg mine-owners from the dynamite monopoly would have been extremely unpopular with the British public. Milner himself found that home opinion was still "dormant" on the subject of South Africa at the beginning of 1899. In the estimation of those whose job it was to know, there was no irresistible urge in British politics or business to conquer the Transvaal. When Milner came home in November 1898 to press for decisive action, he found that "the 'no-war' policy is still in favour in the highest quarters." But he returned to Cape Town in February 1899 thinking that "If I can advance matters by my own actions . . . I shall have support when the time comes." If British opinion still slept, at least the international position had brightened. The crises with France at Fashoda and on the Niger had come and gone. The Chinese crisis was passing. Germany had withdrawn from South African affairs.

But once again it seems to have been the British party in South Africa that forced Chamberlain to turn the screw on Kruger again. Since November 1898, he had suspected that Kruger was coming to a settlement with the Johannesburg mine-owners, in return for a loan. Such a bargain would have reconciled the capitalists without breaching Kruger's *régime* and would have taken the heart out of the reform movement. The Colonial Secretary warned the gold mining houses against "selling [themselves] and the Uitlander position rather cheap." At the same time, the Cape and Free State governments were proposing a conference between the four South African states to smooth their disputes. Chamberlain and Milner did their best to discourage Schreiner's proposal, fearing that it was meant to take the settlement out of imperial hands. In April 1899, Kruger offered the *Uitlanders* comprehensive concessions in the "Great Deal," if they would cease their agitation against the republic in Johannesburg and in London. . . . Chamberlain wished the *Uitlanders* to insist upon full municipal status for Johannesburg. The "Great Deal" failed because of the Reformers' increased demands, and they were joined by the mine-owners in a renewed campaign for the franchise. In the middle of April Chamberlain received their mass petition for imperial aid. Milner implied that an imperial refusal to intervene this time might drive the pro-British parties in South Africa to make their own bargains with the republic. The Colonial Secretary's dilemma of April 1896 and April 1897 had recurred. He was forced to choose between an ultimatum to the republic and antagonising the South African "loyalists." The Cabinet was informed:

Our relations with the Transvaal have again reached a critical stage.

We have to reply to an Uitlander petition of 21,000.

If we ignore altogether the prayer of the petitioners, it is certain that British influence in South Africa will be severely shaken.

If we send an ultimatum to Kruger, it is possible, and in my opinion probable, that we shall get an offensive reply. . . .

We cannot expect any support from the present Cape Government which is a Bond Government with strong leanings towards the Transvaal.

. . . The present state of things is a source of constant danger, and cannot continue indefinitely.

Chamberlain proposed a threatening despatch to Kruger which would stop short of an ultimatum, yet keep the "loyalists" hopes high.

Neither the Colonial Secretary nor the Cabinet in May 1899 were deliberately manoeuvering the republic into war. They feared the outcome of Milner's belligerence. . . . Salisbury's Cabinet felt that Milner and the *Uitlanders* were hurrying them toward an ultimatum which British opinion might think unjustified. The government reluctantly agreed to a diplomatic offensive in support of the reformers' claims, but was still anxious to steer clear of war. It eagerly accepted proposals from the Free State and colonial ministers for negotiations between Kruger and Milner at Bloemfontein.

The High Commissioner demanded the vote for all *Uitlanders* who had resided in the republic for five years, as well as more seats in the Volkraad. Kruger offered a limited seven year franchise. On 5 June, Milner broke up the conference. As he put it, "they want to squeeze the newcomers into the existing mould. I want them to burst it." Chamberlain and his colleagues thought that Milner had been much too abrupt. In mid-July however, Kruger, pressed by the Free State and the colonial governments, at last proposed a law giving substantial concessions to the immigrants. The High Commissioner thought that Kruger was merely playing for time. "No franchise measure should be accepted as satisfactory," he wrote, "unless its provisions are agreed between the two governments and guaranteed by compact between them. This is [the] only chance of obtaining decent measure. . . . To assert our power and retain confidence of loyalists are after all the main objects to keep in view."

Chamberlain on the other hand mistook the new franchise law at first as a sign that Kruger's government was on the run. The Colonial Secretary wrote to Salisbury:

. . . I really am sanguine that the crisis is over. . . . If my expectations are justified by official confirmation tomorrow the result will be a triumph of moral pressure — accompanied by special service officers and 3 Batteries of artillery.

Thus encouraged, Chamberlain seized the opportunity to stretch his advantage further, and assert the imperial authority's right to examine and approve the franchise bill jointly with the republican government. . . . Under the illusion of victory, the Colonial Secretary had changed from defence to attack. Hitherto he had been moved mainly by the need to retain the *Uitlander* and Rhodesian parties' loyalty to the empire. Now Milner felt confident enough to contemplate turning the Transvaal into an English republic. "In forcing S[outh] A[frican] R[epublic] in direction of equal rights and genuine self-government," Chamberlain, as much as Milner, now intended "the practical assertion of British supremacy" in its internal affairs. Exulting over the apparent triumph of moral pressure in the franchise question, he impulsively committed himself and his colleagues to winning back supremacy over the Transvaal by diplomatic force.

By the end of August it was plain that moral pressure was not sufficient to impose the increased imperial demands. But they could not now be withdrawn. There was nothing for it but an ultimatum. Ministers unhappily discussed their mistaken opportunism. Hicks Beach wrote: ". . . I hope Milner and the Uitlanders will not be allowed to drag us into war." The Prime Minister also blamed the High Commissioner and the extreme British party in South Africa.

"The Boers will hate you for a generation, even if they submit," he complained to Lansdowne:

If they resist and are beaten, they will hate you still more. . . . [Milner's] view is too heated, if you consider the intrinsic significance and importance of the things which are in controversy. But it recks little to think of that now. What he has done cannot be effaced. We have to act upon a moral field prepared for us by him and his jingo supporters. And therefore I see before us the necessity for considerable military effort — and all for people whom we despise, and for territory which will bring no profit and no power to England.

The rest of the Cabinet heartily disliked Chamberlain's and Milner's methods. Yet in the end they approved them. They preferred not to drive Chamberlain to resign. It seemed too late to draw back. Above all they agreed that supremacy in South Africa must be regained.

On 28 August Chamberlain replied to the Transvaal's latest offer of a five years retrospective franchise and a quarter of the Volkraad seats for the *Uitlanders*. In return Kruger's executive expected the imperial government to give up its claim to suzerainty, to refer disputes in future to the arbitration of the South African governments, and to stop further intervention in the republic's internal affairs. The British government accepted the franchise and arbitration proposals, but insisted upon its own suzerainty and right of intervention. Required to agree to these imperial terms under threat of an ultimatum, the republic refused to yield; and Chamberlain asked for troops to go to Natal. Since war seemed inevitable, he suggested raising the British terms. Milner and the South African loyalists wanted ". . . to take some security that all the conditions of a settlement [of the Transvaal] shall be observed." On 2 September Chamberlain told the Prime Minister: "I can only think of three ways in which this might be effected, viz., Occupation, Disarmament or Federation, and neither (*sic*) could be secured except as the result of a successful war. . . ."

Chamberlain vehemently argued the necessity of reconquering the Transvaal to save South Africa for the empire. Since a military solution seemed inevitable, he wished to raise Britain's demands on the republic. But Salisbury and Hicks Beach saw no advantage in asking for more, so long as hope of peace remained. On 17 September Kruger's executive rejected the British demands. War seemed unavoidable. The Cabinet agreed to formulate final terms for a settlement to be imposed by ultimatum.

Ministers had not aimed deliberately at provoking war. They had arrived at it with regret and foreboding, while trying to assert a disappearing supremacy. Hicks

Beach probably best expressed their mood on the eve of war:

I am sure . . . that none of us (except possibly J[oseph] C[hamberlain] though I am by no means sure about him) likes the business. But we all feel that it has got to be done — and though I feel grave doubts as to the effects of a war, both in South Africa and on the fortunes of our party here, the Dutch in South Africa can hardly like us less than they do now, and I hope at the end will have learned to respect us.

Salisbury had written in the same vein, and even more pungently. But by now Salisbury was not the ruthless and poised statesman who had presided over the partition. He was growing old. He was failing. Above all his wife was dying, and the Prime Minister was a man of sorrows. He doubted with Hicks Beach whether war would be popular with the British electorate. "Public opinion here," he wrote, "is not very irritable [with the Boers]. . . . Public opinion in South Africa is no doubt rabid. . . ." The government had not been driven into war by imperialist hysteria at Home but by British South African opinion. Ministers all along had believed that Home opinion had to be educated and manufactured to give them support in case of conflict with the Transvaal. Lord James had preferred peace to a war to restore imperial paramountcy. "But at last I was convinced," he admitted, "that the Boer Government meant war."

The ultimatum drafted on 9 October shows what the imperial aims had become, once war was inevitable. A new convention was to provide for the repeal of all legislation since 1881 imposing disabilities upon alien residents of the republic. They were to be reinstated in all the privileges open to them at the time of the retrocession. Full municipal rights were to be granted to the mining districts, and the independence of the courts of justice was to be guaranteed. The republic was to be restricted in its armaments. Upon these conditions the British government offered to guarantee the independence of the republic against external aggression. The essential demand was for equality between the white races in the Transvaal. As Hicks Beach put it:

I see no reason for proposing anything now which would be taken as a revocation of independence. We can never govern from Downing Street any part of South Africa in which the whites are strong enough to defend themselves against the natives: so that equality of white races in the Transvaal would really secure all we can desire, viz. British predominance.

The Colonial Secretary agreed: ". . . we do not want in any case to make ourselves responsible for the Government of the Transvaal." But he added, "It must be a Republic or a self-governing Colony — under the British flag in either case."

But the British ultimatum was never sent. On 9 October, the Transvaal presented its own ultimatum, demanding the withdrawal of British troops from the republic's borders. The Boer war began.

The Threat of an Independent South Africa

J. S. MARAIS

THE advent of Joseph Chamberlain as colonial secretary marked the turning-point in Anglo-Boer relations during the last two decades of the nineteenth century. Up to that point the clash between Britain and the South African Republic had been on the outposts. The outcome of this "battle of the outposts" was the virtual encirclement of the two Boer republics with British territory, and in particular the denial to the Transvaal of access to the sea. There remained the neutral port of Delagoa Bay, but the neutrality of the bay was precarious. When Chamberlain became colonial secretary in 1895 the struggle was transferred to the citadel itself, within which the Trojan horse in the shape of the Uitlander population had been introduced during the preceding decade. Before the end of the year there followed the Jameson raid. To Chamberlain the raid was by no means an unmitigated disaster. "I even regard it as possible," he wrote after the fiasco, "that it may bring matters to a head and lead to the settlement of many pending questions." The question we must try to answer in conclusion is: Which of these "questions" were soluble without war and which insoluble; or in other words, what was the war about?

There are those who have answered the question in accordance with some doctrine of historical determinism. It has been said, for example, that the war was one between the sixteenth (or seventeenth) and the nineteenth (or twentieth) centuries with the implication that it was inevitable. Sir James Rose Innes in his valuable *Autobiography* does not adopt the war-of-the-centuries view, but considers, nevertheless,

that war was inevitable. I do not see how the historian can adopt a determinist standpoint. The "inevitable outcome" is, actually, descried only after it has come about. When it is descried in advance, it usually fails to take place. Determinist history implies in fact a claim to omniscience.

The responsibility for the war has often been laid at the door of the mining magnates. More precisely, it is alleged that they engineered the war for the sake of their dividends. But the interests of these financiers or "capitalists" required certain well-understood reforms in the administration of the republic, not an attack on her independence. For the purpose of promoting these interests united action by the capitalists was desirable and practicable. But it became impracticable when these limits were transgressed. This was one of the lessons driven home by the fiasco of the raid. An important section among the capitalists were altogether opposed to the plan of an armed rebellion, and even among those who supported it there were misgivings about the political aims of their leader, Rhodes. This distrust of Rhodes the statesman contributed its share to the ruin of the enterprise. Yet it remains true that a powerful group of capitalists played a leading and indispensable role in the plot that led to the raid. Chamberlain kept in the background, intending to show his hand only after the capitalists had led Johannesburg into actual revolt.

In the prolonged crisis that culminated in war the roles were reversed. In 1895 Rhodes and a number of Rand capitalists took the lead, but counted on the support of the British government at the critical

From J. S. Marais, *The Fall of Kruger's Republic* (Oxford, 1961), pp. 323–332. Reprinted by permission of The Clarendon Press, Oxford.

moment. The mess they made of the enterprise taught the capitalists their lesson. They withdrew into the shell out of which they had ventured in 1895, and left the political initiative to the British government. As the crisis deepened they emerged out of their shell once more, this time as instruments of British policy. They acted now as men under orders, relying on the superior political wisdom of the professional statesmen.

It was not until late in 1897 that the capitalist front could be effectively reconstituted with the circumscribed object of taking united action in the interests of the mining industry. But in their attitude to the republican government the capitalists continued to differ among themselves. The most important of them, the Wernher-Beit firm, remained uncompromisingly hostile. But certain other big firms did not share this hostility. In January 1899 Milner and Chamberlain took the important step of arranging joint action between themselves and the chamber of mines in opposition to the dynamite monopoly. They were making a bid for the support of the capitalists during the critical months that lay ahead. The bid was sufficiently, if not entirely, successful. The joint action against the dynamite monopoly led directly to the fateful negotiations between the republican government and the capitalists, in which the latter were guided by the advice of the senior partner, the colonial office. But even at this juncture, the capitalists were not unanimous. They could not agree on the demands to be made on Kruger. It was not only "foreign" firms like those of Goerz and Albu that were unwilling to ask too much, but also a "British" firm like the Consolidated Goldfields. It was partly due to his awareness of this fact that Fitzpatrick broke up the negotiations and handed over the job to the British government. When the latter took over, the capitalists retired into the background. Those of them who did not agree with the British government's policy were prepared to acquiesce under the combined pressure of the colonial office and Wernher, Beit & Company.

II

A well-known historian declared recently: "The essential British problem in South Africa was strategical and political, not economic. . . . The British needed a united white South Africa in order to have strategic security at the Cape — the lynchpin of the British Empire. . . . The naval station at the Cape was . . . fundamental to them. . . ." Though British statesmen undoubtedly attached great importance to the naval base at Simonstown, it is not clear why a united South Africa was necessary for the security of the base. The British garrison and naval squadron provided an effective enough guarantee. The game that was played in South Africa in the 1890's was for other stakes than the security of Simonstown. In the eyes of British statesmen a united South Africa — like a united Canada and a united Australia — would be a source of additional strength to the British empire instead of a source of expense. It is true that Lord Salisbury appears not to have agreed with this view, but Salisbury was in a minority in his cabinet.

"No one," writes professor C. W. de Kiewiet, "who has read . . . the records of British policy since the achievement of Confederation in Canada can miss the picture of a British Government groping for some means of ending South African disunity." So far, so good. But he then goes on to write as if he had adopted as his major premiss the theory that the political federation of South Africa was an historical necessity. It is an assumption that lies at the base of a great deal of South African historiography. Those who write history in this way naturally conclude that the opponents of federation could not but be swept aside, since they had placed themselves athwart the destiny of South Africa. But I have said already that the historian cannot steer by the light of a determinist philosophy.

It was the Great Trek of the 1830's that was responsible for South African disunity. The British government was naturally reluctant to acquiesce in the birth of a second source of "White" political power in South Africa. It took that government the best part of twenty years to make up its mind to recognize the independence of two Boer states in the interior, and then only after annexing the coastal republic of Natal and in the confident anticipation that the inland states would remain of small account, if indeed they managed to maintain themselves at all in the face of internal dissensions and Native hostility. But what if the new states survived and grew in strength? The only step taken by the British government in the early days to insure itself against such an eventuality was to veto a union between the two republics. It was a significant step; but it did not go far enough since it failed to forestall an inter-republican alliance. The next step, taken much later, was to propose a South African federation under the British flag. But two successive attempts to put the plan into practice encountered armed resistance and by 1896 — after the failure of the second attempt — the prospects looked particularly unpromising.

Federation was the ideal solution, but it might not be attainable. The British authorities felt therefore that they had to provide some alternative answer to the problem of the duality of political power (or will) in South Africa. They found the answer in the concept of paramountcy or supremacy. British paramountcy proved to be an elastic term, but even in its mildest interpretation it meant the denial of full republican independence. The republics, and more particularly the Orange Free State, got an unmistakable taste of paramountcy when the British, after intervening in quarrels between the latter state and independent Native chiefs north of the Orange, annexed both the territory of Basutoland and the diamond fields of Griqualand West (1868–71). The annexation of the South African Republic in 1877

was a vigorous demonstration of paramountcy, undertaken with a view to South African federation. When the republic was restored in 1884, certain limits were set to its independence particularly in regard to treaty-making power. But the claim to paramountcy, while it included and was partly expressed in these legal limitations, was not exhausted by them.

That the British authorities, speaking in the name of a powerful empire, should assert their paramountcy over two republics struggling to find their feet was natural. It was equally natural that the republics should oppose the claim. Having undertaken the responsibilities of independence, they claimed also its rights. It was not really a question of petty African communities claiming to be "ordinary European states." It was a question rather of the meaning of political independence. (This is not to deny that it was in fact European jurists and statesmen who were the creators of modern international law — not, however, for Europe only but for the world.) As for paramountcy, the republics did not formally repudiate the claim as an abstract proposition. But they protested whenever its application affected their interests. They did not, however, carry their protests to the length of armed resistance except in the case of the annexation of the South African Republic.

III

When it had become clear by 1895 that the gold-fields of the Witwatersrand had vast potentialities, the problem of the duality of political power began, in the eyes of British statesmen, to take on a new urgency. Writing to Chamberlain late in 1896 on "the South African question" Selborne remarked:

In a generation the S.A.R. will by its wealth and population dominate South Africa. South African politics must revolve round the Transvaal, which will be the only possible market for the agricultural produce or the manufactures of Cape Colony and Natal. The commercial attraction of the

Transvaal will be so great that a Union of the South African States with it will be absolutely necessary for their prosperous existence. The only question in my opinion is whether that Union will be inside or outside the British Empire.

About two years later Milner expressed the fear "that the overwhelming preponderance in wealth and opportunity on the side of the Transvaal may turn the scale against us." As for Chamberlain, he publicly warned the two republican presidents in 1897 against aspiring to an independent federation.

The colonial office had in its files many warnings that Britain might lose the loyalty of the British settlers not only in the Transvaal but throughout South Africa. Rhodes had sent such a warning shortly after the raid. Greene sent another early in April 1897. He was describing a dinner party given by Abe Bailey, one of Johannesburg's mining magnates. Jorissen of the republican bench urged those present "to join him in an attempt . . . to frame a new Constitution which would give the Uitlanders all the rights they wanted," including a seven years' retrospective franchise, on condition that they "renounced allegiance to the land of their birth and agreed to accept the Transvaal as their own country." Most of Jorissen's hearers thought that he spoke with the knowledge of his government.

The judge's advice to the Uitlanders [continued Greene] to renounce their nationality, and rely on the good faith of the Government of the Republic, could only, I think, be intended as a bait to induce them to abate their confidence in the Imperial Government. At present, in consequence of the recent public utterances of the Secretary of State . . . , the Imperial feeling on the Rand is growing in strength; but when we consider that a considerable proportion of the community entertain a certain misgiving as to the thoroughness of Imperial policy . . . a movement such as that advocated by . . . Jorissen might find some . . . support.

At about the same time J. W. Leonard, a leading Johannesburg Uitlander and at one time attorney-general of the Cape Colony, declared in an interview reported to the colonial office: "It is essential that England should re-establish her lost prestige in South Africa. This is the last chance she will have of retaining the loyalty of Englishmen and others . . . in the country. . . . Kruger would welcome the support of such men gladly, provided that he was convinced that they had thrown over England. A little time back he sent me a message offering to make me attorney-general of the Transvaal on that condition."

The determination to forestall an independent United States of South Africa lies at the root of British policy after the proving of the deep levels on the Rand. The longer the South African Republic retained her independence the greater seemed the risk that the British colonies would be attracted away from the empire. For some time after the raid there was not much the British authorities could do to checkmate the republic. Their first opportunity to assert themselves came in April 1897. The April demonstration was followed within six months by the assertion of suzerainty. Suzerainty was intended to underpin or legalize paramountcy, and to issue in complete British control over the republic's foreign relations. If this could be achieved the danger of the republic's taking the lead in the formation of an independent federation would be considerably reduced.

The danger might be reduced; it would not be eliminated. It would persist as long as the republican government was a Boer government. It would in fact persist as long as the republic, whether her government were Boer or Uitlander, remained outside the empire. Indeed, it was the prevailing opinion in the colonial office, until Milner appeared on the scene, that it would not be in the interests of Britain to convert the Boer state into an Uitlander republic owing to the risk that the latter would be a more efficient nucleus of an independent federation. Chamberlain himself shared this opinion.

Milner's importance lies in the fact that

he converted the colonial office to his solution of the "duality" problem. He did not fear a republic which admitted the Uitlanders to citizenship. On the contrary he held that she would become a part of the empire, provided that Britain obtained complete political equality for the new citizens without delay and at the same time mastered the republican will to independence.

But if the republican will to independence was not mastered, what would then be the ultimate outcome? Undoubtedly, declared Milner, an independent Republic of South Africa (though the British naval base at Simonstown would be secure for a long time). We have seen that this was also Selborne's view. Milner, however, was the man on the spot and he undertook to enlighten the colonial office on the inwardness of the situation. He came to the conclusion that the independence of the South African Republic was incompatible with the interests of Britain because the republic was the prime cause of the growth of Afrikaner nationalism throughout South Africa. Afrikaner nationalism was the real enemy. What was this Afrikaner nationalism of the late 1890's? Its portrait as painted by Milner looks remarkably like the visage it wears today when it has grown to full stature as the result of the Anglo-Boer war and an effort extending over half a century. A nationalist himself, he recognized the symptoms of a malady to which the patient was not to succumb until many years later.

Milner was not interested in the purely cultural aspect of Afrikaner nationalism. It was the political aspect that worried him. "The Afrikander Nation idea," if it ever came to fruition, meant political independence. "To afrikanderize" meant to him to become "a virtual Republican." This explains how he could lump together all the Cape opponents of his policy — starting from staunch supporters of the imperial connexion like de Villiers and Schreiner and continuing via Hofmeyr, who had no objection in principle to the British flag, to out-and-out republican members of the Afrikaner bond — as the Afrikaner or Dutch party. It appeared to him that even the "imperialists" among his opponents, in their solicitude for the interests of South Africa and their fear of the disastrous after-effects of war, were willing to take a chance with regard to the imperial connexion. This he was not prepared to do. (In any case he thought that the after-effects of war would be good.) Whether at the cost of war or not it was his firm resolve to secure South Africa's connexion with the empire for ever. That is the explanation of his desire to see the "Afrikander Nation idea" doomed. That explains also what he meant when he spoke of "the great game between ourselves and the Transvaal for the mastery in South Africa." He meant that unless the republic changed its character, its assertion of independence would be copied sooner or later by the rest of South Africa. But the transformation would have to be quick and radical. That was the reason why he insisted that the Uitlanders should be admitted to the republican franchise, not in gradually increasing numbers, but "wholesale" and on an equal footing with the Boers. If the former course was followed the Uitlanders might "afrikanderize," i.e. become supporters of republican independence. If they were admitted "wholesale" by the action of Britain, they would "burst the existing mould" and the republic would cease to have a will of her own.

IV

The republican government realized too late what it meant to have Chamberlain as a challenger. If it had appreciated its peril, it might sooner have taken appropriate action. As things turned out, the republican record with regard to reform was one of procrastination. The procrastination can be explained. But the fact remains that it was fatal. By the end of 1898 the final crisis had overtaken the republic. Yet as late as the end of April 1899 Smuts still believed that Britain would not go to war unless she had a formally good *casus belli*.

As British policy gradually unfolded during the succeeding months, the republican leaders came to the conclusion that Britain was aiming a mortal blow at their independence. Once they had reached that conclusion, they decided to fight. They believed that they stood a chance of winning, especially if they could strike before the British were ready. In spite of a discouraging report from Leyds late in September, they hoped for foreign intervention. Even if they did not win, they may have hoped that Salisbury's government would fall if they held out long enough, and a more sympathetic government take its place. But calculations such as these do not constitute the reason why the republics went to war. After the outbreak of war de Villiers wrote: "With these people the preservation of their independence is a sacred mission." Up to the very end he had urged the republicans to give way if they could do so "without actual dishonour." Shortly before the Bloemfontein conference his brother Melius wrote to him: "Men like Mr. Hofmeyr also to some extent forget that the S.A.R. like the Free State has a certain measure of self-respect. . . ." On 16 September the government of the South African Republic sent Hofmeyr its last word: "We are fully impressed with the very serious position in which we are placed, but with God before our eyes we cannot go further, without endangering, if not totally destroying, our independence. This Government, Parliament and people are unanimous on this point." The Free Staters' last word had already been spoken by Fischer: "We have honestly done our best, and can do no more. If we are to lose our independence, since that is what is demanded, leave us at all events the consolation that we did not sacrifice it dishonourably."

VII. CAUSED BY PERSONALITIES?

Any study of the Anglo-Boer War must focus to a considerable extent on the two leading personalities, Chamberlain and Milner, who, in their respective posts stood at the very center of events, each a molder of policy. Joseph Chamberlain was fortunate in having J. L. Garvin as his biographer. Editor for thirty-four years of *The Observer* — a post in which he wielded remarkable influence — and also editor of the fourteenth edition of the *Encyclopaedia Britannica*, Mr. Garvin was given access to the Chamberlain papers. He lived to complete three volumes of a remarkable full-length biography; a fourth was later written by Mr. Julian Amery. Garvin, who is a staunch defender of the Colonial Secretary, includes in his biography lengthy passages from Chamberlain's speeches and letters. The first reading below presents a picture of Chamberlain's role in the critical summer of 1899.

The Milner Papers, from which the final reading is chosen, deserve a high place among records left by modern political figures. Milner possessed abilities of a high order, and he had a varied career. After a brilliant record at Oxford, he served for a few years on the *Pall Mall Gazette*, where he shared W. T. Stead's enthusiasm for social reform. But the passion of his life was public service. He gained administrative experience under Lord Cromer in Egypt and wrote a significant book on Britain's role there, *England in Egypt* (1892). Subsequently, with approval from all sides, Milner succeeded Lord Rosmead as High Commissioner in South Africa, a post at which he served for eight years (1897–1905), playing a key role in the negotiations of 1899 and in post-war reconstruction. His devotion to the cause of imperial union is well-known. During World War I he served as a member of the War Cabinet, and in 1918 helped to arrange the appointment of Foch instead of Pétain as coordinator on the Western Front. His dispatches are remarkable for lucidity and for their frank expression of his views. They constitute the most revealing single source on the coming of the Anglo-Boer War.

Chamberlain — A Wise and Resourceful Statesman?

J. L. GARVIN

CHAMBERLAIN's dispatch of May 10 accepting on behalf of Her Majesty's Government the Uitlanders' Petition to the Queen was published at last; and likewise the blue-book containing Milner's burning advocacy of the case for the "Helots." It was the talk of the nation. Opinion was divided in the manner already depicted. The Cape Dutch were infuriated against the High Commissioner at a moment when between him and the Afrikander leaders negotiations of a kind were still going on. The leader of the Opposition gave the first signal that in case of war the Government could not count on his support. Chamberlain's private representations to Sir Henry Campbell-Bannerman were fruitless.

The Colonial Secretary was blamed even by some of Milner's friends for what they called the premature publication of the philippic against Kruger's oppression. Now, the "Helots" dispatch was written for almost immediate publicity as we know, but because of the Bloemfontein Conference it had been already for six weeks withheld.

Meanwhile, what had been happening at Pretoria? President Kruger laid before the Volksraad the draft of a new franchise law embodying with some improvements his propositions at Bloemfontein. The draft purported to reduce the franchise period from fourteen years to seven. He declared that to give away more would give away independence. He did not want war, but at need the Lord who had watched over them in the past would be their stay. The Uitlanders insist that the restrictions make a mockery of the Bill. The Colonial Secretary urges that the Cape Premier should press Kruger to improve the Bill. The High Commissioner for his part has no faith in Afrikander mediation nor in anything but a British ultimatum. It would bring all waverers to the British side. "The most probable result would be a complete climb-down on part of S.A.R. and if not that a war, which, however deplorable in itself, would at least enable us to put things on a sound basis for the future better than even the best-devised Convention can." With accentuated optimism this is but a new version of Milner's old thesis, "Reform or War." It was easier to repeat it on paper than for statesmen to grapple with it amidst the democratic divisions of the Mother Country.

Thus the controversy worked back to the question of Chamberlain's personality and management. Did he retain his old powers of command in the country? If so when and how would he exert them?

By comparison with British excitement in South Africa British feeling at home was not in marching order. Fervent Imperialists, convinced that it would and must come to war with the Boers, and so the sooner the better, were in a minority though strong. Many Conservatives as well as Liberals were puzzled and checked by the new complications and subtleties of the franchise controversy. To them the difference between a five years' franchise and a seven years' seemed little more than the difference between tweedledum and tweedledee. What was this to make a war of? Few grasped what was the real alter-

From J. L. Garvin, *The Life of Joseph Chamberlain*, III (London, 1934), pp. 412–417; 424–427; 433–441. Reprinted by permission of Macmillan & Co., Ltd.

native raised by the network of restrictions and precautions devised at Pretoria. The choice lay between prolonged exclusion of all but a modicum of the Uitlanders and immediate admission of the larger number.

The Colonial Secretary's discriminating eye — in these matters the most experienced of all eyes — saw well that public opinion would require masterly handling. The contrast between his sinewy gradualness and Milner's ardent chafing would have to continue for some time.

Psychologically, there is perhaps no more interesting study in Chamberlain's career. He desired peace if possible. But there must be some wide redress in the Transvaal. In case of war he would have to bear the brunt of the political storm. He would be hated as even he had not been hated. It behoved him to make no slip such as might be his political undoing. He made none.

By arrangement made long before he was engaged to address the annual Liberal Unionist gathering in Birmingham Town Hall. The occasion was fixed for a date three weeks after the Bloemfontein breakup. To Milner and his near friends the time seemed long. When the Birmingham meeting was near, Lord Selborne, second in command at the Colonial Office, made an extreme personal appeal to its chief. If the Government continued to seem weak and dilatory, Milner and perhaps others would resign. We would avert war by facing it, but bring it by fumbling. The Opposition would try to give the Colonial Secretary a heavy throw whatever he did. Surely it was time to tell the country that British predominance was at stake in South Africa and to convince Kruger that "the Cabinet mean business this time, once and for all."

Chamberlain's answer was one of the few letters of his that show all the man in his nerve and circumspection when he had perilous business on hand. No one alive could give him lessons in either of two things — courage of purpose and skill in approach.

CHAMBERLAIN TO SELBORNE

June 23, 1899. — Many thanks. My speech was finally settled — subject to possible telegrams — before I got your letter. I think it will fairly meet your wishes.

The difficulty — which only presents itself in full force to those who are actually responsible — is not so much to make up one's own mind as to keep perfect faith with one's colleagues and friends.

I have no idea that in this case they will differ from me, but the more loyal they are the more I am bound not to commit them further than they have agreed to go.

I don't care a twopenny damn for office, or for the temporary gusts of public opinion.

In any course there is risk, as Mr. Kruger is a very uncertain factor, but I hope to get my way in the long run, and, provided that we do not recede an inch, we may be satisfied now and then to dawdle.

There is no doubt that opinion in the House of Commons is fluid, and on the whole, I think, bad. Perhaps they will rise to my fly — perhaps they won't.

I want to get the water into good condition; and to do everything *selon les règles*. Then if I fail, *"Victrix causa diis placuit sed victa Catoni"* — Yours ever, CATO.

None the less he thinks as on some occasions before, but this time a little grimly, that the High Commissioner is remote from appreciation of political difficulties at home. For all the staunch defence he has framed, he minutes with regard to its subject: "Milner is really rather trying. . . . I shall do my best for Milner, and for the policy which is mine as well as his, to-morrow — but he is overstrained."

On the night the Town Hall was crammed in the Birmingham spirit. Large numbers were turned away. The crowd within would have been doubled or more had space allowed. Listeners who often had heard him thought the speech one of the finest they had known — "sober, earnest, clear," said his wife. It earned those words. As so often before in the same scene he excelled in the steady marshalling of his case and carried his audience with him by the compacted sentences and their consecutive march. He showed how the reconciling intentions of Gladstone's Government in 1881 and 1884 had been frustrated; how since then the spirit of the London Convention, so far as it meant to provide for the equal rights of non-Boer inhabitants and new settlers, had been violated and reversed. We had been four times on the verge of war with the Transvaal:

Whatever we may think of the original policy, we must admit that its results have disappointed the hopes of all those who were the prominent advocates of its adoption. . . . All the grievances of the Outlanders, of which you hear so much, date from the second Convention of 1884. . . . In 1881 when the Convention was being discussed, President Kruger was asked by our representatives what treatment would be given to British subjects in the Transvaal. He said, "All strangers have now and will always have equal rights and privileges with the burghers of the Transvaal," and yet . . . the majority of the population of the Transvaal, which consists of these same strangers chiefly British subjects, have no representation, although they have made the prosperity of the State, and although they pay five-sixths of the revenue.

He upheld the High Commissioner:

We selected Sir Alfred Milner. We sent him out because we believed that he was the best man to deal with this difficult situation, and now that he is there in the midst of intrigue and hatred we intend to support him. . . . I am abused — for what, ye gods should I not be abused! — . . . because I published his despatch which was sent to me for publication. What would have been said if I had withheld it?

The concluding passages meant that there would be no flaunting but no flinching.

Those who say that there is a party within the Government that desires war are guilty of a mischievous untruth. On the other hand, those fall into a grievous error who think that there is a party within the Government who having put their hands to the plough will now draw back. . . . We will not be hurried on the one hand; we will not be held back on the other. But having undertaken this business we will see it through.

Telling again were his few words in reply to the vote of thanks:

I have spoken to you from my heart tonight. I believe that we have reached a critical, and a turning, point in the history of the Empire. I think our Colonies, and, indeed, I might almost say the nations of the world, are watching us in a difficulty which may well try the temper and character of our people—watching to see how we shall emerge from it.

Always in crisis Chamberlain stamped a phrase or two upon the popular mind. Now, we had "put our hands to the plough", and "having undertaken this business we will see it through". This speech went far to convince the majority of the country — still desiring peace with reform like Chamberlain himself — that war might have to be waged. The overseas empire was widely stirred; the ideal of racial equality appealed straight to Canada and Australia. In Her Majesty's own hand came his commendation: "The Queen greatly admires Mr. Chamberlain's speech". Queen Victoria had commanded Miss Phipps, her reader, to read it out to her and had listened to every word of it with the closest attention. George Wyndham wrote off, a few days later: "Things are going very well here. Chamberlain's speech has done wonders. Lord Lansdowne and Ritchie both told me they thought it excellent, and on the slow-thinking mass of M.P.'s the effect has been beyond hope. They wanted a lead and now having got one they are prepared to follow."

*   *   *

The chief debate of the session took place in both Houses on Friday, July 28. It was awaited with intense feeling. Most eagerly by those who expected the subtle satire or cryptic moderation of a pacific Prime Minister at the expense of a belligerent Colonial Minister. We know how foolish was this partisan hypothesis. Those who entertained it were confounded.

Salisbury's comments were more drastic than any yet heard from his chief colleague. The Convention had been used, he said, "to reduce the English to the condition almost of a conquered, certainly of a subjugated, race." He implied that if war came, the Republic would be annexed. "If it ever happens that the validity of these Conventions is impeached, I believe they belong from that time entirely to history." The Prime Minister closed with Chamberlain's symbol, "We have put our hands to the plough . . ."

The House of Commons, benches crowded below and galleries above, bore the aspect of a great sitting. The leader of the Opposition, Campbell-Bannerman, opened by admitting that the Uitlander grievances constituted "a constant source of danger to the peace and prosperity of all the States and colonies in South Africa." He hoped that the franchise qualification would be further reduced to less than seven years; but the difference between seven and five was nothing to fight about; patience might well obliterate even that difference; no excuse remained for war or for talk of war.

The Colonial Secretary's immediate reply traversed the whole case. Delivered throughout in his own terse clear-cut manner, it was nothing if not moderate. More moderate in word and inference than the Prime Minister's style in another place. "No one dreams of acquiring this country which we of our free will retroceded. No one has any wish whatever to interfere with the independence we have granted. . . . We desire to place it on a firm basis by turning discontented aliens into loyal fellow-citizens of the Dutch." But the present "humiliating inferiority" of British subjects in the Transvaal could not long remain unremedied without raising greater issues — the predominance of Great Britain in South Africa, the peace of South Africa. There was no trivial quarrel about a mere difference between a seven years' and a five years' franchise. That point was a quibble.

The real matter to elucidate was whether the nominal Seven Years Bill did in fact give any kind of "immediate and substantial representation". There must be "some approach in practice" to "equality of condition between the two white races."

Without this the Transvaal will remain what it is at present — a source of unrest, disturbance and danger. Although the situation is an anxious one I am hopeful of the future. I am hopeful for two reasons. In the first place because . . . President Kruger has, I believe, come to the conclusion that the Government are in earnest and that they have the people behind them. I trust under these circumstances to his common-sense. I trust to his present knowledge that reforms are necessary and I hope we may be able to convince him in any further negotiations and communications that we do not seek to do him or his country any harm but rather to help him to maintain his position and his authority, whilst at the same time securing justice to all the inhabitants of the country. But I am hopeful for a second reason, and that is because I have an absolute conviction that the great mass of the people of this country are prepared to support us, if the necessity should arise, in any measures we may think it necessary to take to secure justice to the British subjects in the Transvaal, and the due observance of the promises and Conventions upon which the independence of the Transvaal has been founded.

Chamberlain had spoken for rather over an hour. Many Liberals as well as the Unionist majority felt, as one of his hearers said, that he had "broken the backbone of the attack."

Both the Prime Minister and the Colonial Secretary anticipated a peaceful solution. They had private reasons. All their information before the debate confirmed a telegram just received from the High Commissioner. It reported a growing opinion that Pretoria and its sympathisers "are still bluffing and will yield further if pressure is kept up. . . ."

But by now, the solid majority of the nation, as Chamberlain well knew, were undoubtedly behind a policy which they held both reasonable and resolute. His consummate management of time had succeeded where a premature offensive such as Milner's school desired would have failed. The British people in the main had come in their way to the conclusion that the South African dispute must be settled soon by agreement or by arms.

*   *   *

On Sunday August 13 all Pretoria was excited. President Kruger and his officials that morning were shut up for two hours in the telegraph office. They were exchanging messages with Bloemfontein. What did it mean? First rumours said it meant immediate war — that the Boer Executive, alarmed at British movements on the border, were determined not to wait. But it was nearly two months yet before the rains would freshen the veldt for the horses.

In fact, this Sabbath telegraphing was concerned with new negotiations. What had happened? The day before, Conyngham Greene, British Agent at Pretoria, had been approached by a member of the Boer Government. Its emissary was its youngest and most brilliant member, Jan Smuts, since world-famous. He had qualifications possessed by no one else. He had won notable honours at Cambridge. The English liked him, and he them as much as the situation allowed. There were no illusions on either side. Not yet thirty, he had the root of statesmanship in him, though if it came to fighting he would be amongst the foremost. Acrid controversy arose out of the pourparlers thus begun. Misunderstandings and recriminations of that kind belong invariably to the preliminaries of war.

Following his first hints of a possible eirenicon, Smuts returned on this Sunday evening with proposals astonishing to the British Agent. They were put forward to exclude and replace the Mixed Commission. On this condition Pretoria would remove every pretext for war. As regards the Uitlanders, Milner's own claim at Bloemfontein would be adopted and improved.

What were the Smuts proposals?

1. A five years' retrospective franchise which might become law in a fortnight.
2. As to representation, just over a quarter of the seats in the Volksraad. This proportion never to be reduced.
3. New burghers to have equal rights in the election of the President and Commandant-General.
4. The details of the new franchise law to be discussed with the British Agent, who may have his legal adviser.
5. The present intervention of Her Majesty's Government not to be a precedent.— No further British insistence on suzerainty, "the controversy on this subject being tacitly allowed to drop." — "Lastly arbitration, from which foreign element is excluded, to be conceded as soon as franchise scheme has become law.

So far, all was radiant. The British Agent's breath was taken away for a moment. Recovering it, he entered into human conversation. Little wonder that, speaking for himself, he went "much too far" — as the High Commissioner thought and told the Colonial Office — in expressing his satisfaction and hope.

I have said as regards suzerainty that I feel sure H. M. Government will not and cannot abandon the right which the preamble to the Convention of 1881 gives them, but that they will have no desire to hurt Boer susceptibilities by publicly reasserting it, so long as no reason to do so is given them by the Government of the S.A.R.

As regards arbitration, they are willing that we should have any of our own judges or lawyers, English or Colonial, to represent us, and that the President or Umpire should be equally English, Colonial or Boer. . . .

As regards suggested possibility of further Conference, State Attorney anticipates that this may now be allowed to lapse.

As regards language, the new members of the Volksraad would use their own.

From Pretoria Greene sent two telegrams in immediate succession. The High Commissioner transmitted each exactly as it was received. One contained the definite memorandum which had been initialed by

Smuts. The other reported the conversational ideas which were not binding. There was nothing to indicate that difference. The Colonial Office took them as successive sheets of a single telegram; and so Chamberlain read them. Disquieted by a bare summary of the first portion only, he had come up from Highbury to London. Then? A genuine five years' franchise and arbitration without foreign interference? It bettered dreams. So far from thinking, with the High Commissioner, that Greene had gone too far in unbosoming himself cordially to Smuts, the Colonial Secretary bluntly instructed Milner to be conciliatory in his turn.

CHAMBERLAIN TO MILNER

August 16.—If proposals now made through British Agent are duly authorised they evidently constitute an immense concession and even a considerable advance on your Bloemfontein proposals. I think it will be a great advantage to get this offer formally made in writing. From the moment you get the note the whole of the negotiations will be direct between the two Governments. . . . Meanwhile, we must obtain official confirmation of proposals and you must avoid any language which would lead S.A.R. to think that we are determined to pick a quarrel. Instruct British Agent at once in accordance with above.

In the same vein, both happy and business-like, the Colonial Secretary informed the Prime Minister:

CHAMBERLAIN TO SALISBURY

Colonial Office, August 16, 1899. — I came up to town to-day on an incomplete abstract of the enclosed telegram and with the impression that some serious step would have to be taken at once.

I was very much relieved to find that the full message seems to give assurance of another climb-down on the part of Kruger which as far as I can see is really complete. . . .

Milner's account is a little alarming and he seems to me unnecessarily suspicious and pedantic in his adherence to form.

I think, however, that he must understand my telegram and see how important I consider it to be that the Boers should not be snubbed at this stage but rather encouraged to put their concessions on record. . . .

The Prime Minister is equally relieved, but — like most of the Cabinet for a long time — less favourable to Milner.

SALISBURY TO CHAMBERLAIN

August 17. — I congratulate you on this telegram, which is very satisfactory. I agree in your criticism of Milner's comment. It looks as if he had been spoiling for the fight with some glee and does not like putting his clothes on again.

How utterly different is all this from many fond accounts of the Unionist Cabinet as with few exceptions a crew of ramping Jingoes — Chamberlain the chief war-dancer. For more than a generation, to the prejudice of Britain and the Empire, that caricature has been credited and disseminated by Liberal attacks, Afrikander repetitions and foreign historians.

Milner proved right in his grimmer conviction. The new hope collapsed.

The breakdown was caused by some change of mind — never yet fully explained — on the Boer side. Here let us have precision about dates. On Saturday, August 19, Kruger's official propositions were delivered. They differed only a little, though thus much for the worse, from the Smuts memorandum. But on Monday, August 21, further reservations destroyed the basis of the overtures. The tone was hard, almost dictatorial.

Franchise and representation for the Uitlanders were made *"expressly conditional"* upon preliminary assurances from the Queen's Government on three points:

"(*a*) In future not to interfere in internal affairs of the South African Republic.

"(*b*) Not to insist further on its assertion of existence of suzerainty.

"(*c*) To agree to arbitration."

This ill-omened message was not an amendment but a revoke. As in the Ems dispatch, a *chamade* had been followed by a *fan-faronnade* — a parley had been changed to a challenge.

To the British Agent came from Smuts a note like a knell: "I do not believe that there is the slightest chance of an alteration or amplification. . . . It will be necessary therefore for you to arrive at your decision on the terms stated as they stand." The date of this moral ultimatum must be well noted. It was August 25. It was the darkest date in the history of South Africa. The Boer ruler and his colleagues well knew in their hearts that they had presented terms which the British Government could not yield.

Kruger had clinched Chamberlain's will. Except when the London Convention was infringed, he had sought peace without swerving for more than three and a half years since the Raid. Now he recognised, once and for all, that his policy of "exhausting the resources of moral pressure" was itself exhausted. With the best attribute of a strong Minister, he, the soul of courage, had not feared to be called weak. Now the other side of a man whom no one ever under-estimated with impunity would re-appear. . . .

Next day in these holiday circumstances of a shining summer the Colonial Secretary made a short, clanging speech addressed both to Britain and the Transvaal. It startled the nation and the Empire and was heard all over the world. Besieged by requests to give a public lead, he had hitherto declined. "It was an awkward moment," as he said in private. Now he felt it was high time to break silence and to use unmistakeable words. He was sure that he had the weight of the country at his back. Messages from Canada, Australia and elsewhere made him as sure of the Empire as a whole.

It was an odd occasion for a mortal warning. He had arranged some time before to throw open his grounds to the Liberal Unionists of Saint Bartholomew's Ward on Saturday, August 26. They had a bright afternoon for their garden party. During a break in the sports he stood on a grassy rise

and addressed his audience in words that some thought impromptu. Not so. They were well considered as the compact phrasing showed. After a little pleasantry suited to the festival, his theme became ominous — that President Kruger had it still in his power to make an honourable and peaceable settlement, but the eleventh hour had struck. "The sands were running down in the glass."

We have been, as you know, negotiating for the last three months with President Kruger. . . . Mr. Kruger procrastinates in his replies. He dribbles out reforms like water from a squeezed sponge and he either accompanies his offers with conditions which he knows to be impossible, or he refuses to allow us to make a satisfactory investigation of the nature and the character of those reforms. . . .

The issues of peace and war are in the hands of President Kruger and of his advisers. . . . Will he speak the necessary words? The sands are running down in the glass. The situation is too fraught with danger, it is too strained for any indefinite postponement to be tolerated. The knot must be loosened, to use Mr. Balfour's words, or else we shall have to find other ways of untying it.

And if we do that, if we are forced to that, then I would repeat now the warning that was given by Lord Salisbury in the House of Lords and I would say that if we are forced to make further preparations, and if this delay continues much longer, we shall not hold ourselves limited by what we have already offered. . . . And if it should come to this — if the rupture which we have done everything in our power to avoid should be forced upon us — I am confident we shall have the support of the vast majority of the people of the United Kingdom, and I will go further and say of the vast majority of the people of the British Empire. . . .

The ring of a voice cannot carry further than this went. Chamberlain could not reveal his knowledge that "take it or leave it" was the latest message of the Transvaal Government. At that eleventh hour the force of his admonition was more necessary than the country could yet be allowed to know. The general tone is measured. One metaphor was assailed by his opponents and justly criticised by many Unionists. Personal satire likening Kruger to a "squeezed sponge" ought to have been omitted from any declaration upon a choice between peace and war. But to say that "the sands were running down in the glass" was not only good English; no figure of language could be closer to the truth as we have seen it to stand.

Two days later, amidst the hubbub about the Highbury speech, the Colonial Secretary addressed to Pretoria a dispatch designedly most mild. He had shown the iron hand; he drew on again the velvet glove. This method before coming to final issues had always been his characteristic. He was set to put his claim so low that if the Transvaal refused, or resorted once more to dilatory indefiniteness, his own fighting position would be impregnable.

What did he do? He assumed that the large immediate enfranchisement proposed by Milner at Bloemfontein would now be conceded in any case. Instead of joint enquiry, though unable to appreciate the objections to it, he would be content that the British Agent with assistants should make examination and report. He hoped that the Transvaal Government would wait for the results of this procedure and that amending suggestions, if required, would be met with a friendly mind. So much for the franchise. What of the stipulations by the Transvaal on the other questions? On them too the dispatch was a pattern of moderation. In effect he said that the Queen's Ministers desired nothing more than to shun avoidable interference with Transvaal affairs. And this, if only the Boers and the Liberal Opposition at home could have realised it, was true.

. . . First, as regards intervention: Her Majesty's Government hope that the fulfilment of the promises made and the just treatment of the Uitlanders in future will render unnecessary any further intervention on their behalf, but Her Majesty's Government cannot of course debar themselves from their rights under the Conventions, nor divest themselves of the ordinary obligations of a civilised Power to protect its subjects in a foreign country from injustice.

Secondly, with regard to suzerainty, Her Majesty's Government would refer the Government of the South African Republic to the second paragraph of my despatch of 13th July. [Stating they had no wish to continue the etymological controversy with the Transvaal, whose claim, however, to be a Sovereign International State, "is not in their opinion warranted either by law or history and is wholly inadmissible."]

Thirdly, Her Majesty's Government agree to a discussion of the form and scope of a Tribunal of Arbitration from which foreigners and foreign influence are excluded. . . .

To hot Unionists this dispatch after the strong stuff of the Highbury speech was another mystifying weakness. They knew nothing of the very man or his methods. He was the same in action as in speaking, when he always lowered his voice before a dangerous passage. Simultaneously with the mild dispatch he sent a private telegram to Milner. It was the Highbury speech itself compressed into a very few formidable lines:

CHAMBERLAIN TO MILNER

August 28. — British Agent may inform State Secretary as his own opinion based on Lord Salisbury's reference to Sibylline books and speech of Secretary of State at Birmingham on Saturday, that if reply to last telegram from H. M. Government is not prompt and satisfactory and if it becomes necessary to despatch further troops, H. M. Government will feel justified in withdrawing previous suggestions for compromise and will formulate their own demands for a settlement.

This is a capital piece in the present book. The Colonial Secretary was at Highbury and his colleagues were dispersed. He felt so certain of himself and of the course now to be taken that without consultation he had fixed the policy to which the Cabinet must come. The next thing was to bring them to it.

From this point, before we come to the play of real forces in the last weeks of nominal peace, the course of diplomacy must be swiftly sketched. Regretting that their recent terms had not found acceptance, the Boer Government withdrew the offer of reform on the Bloemfontein basis. They reverted to the seven years' franchise law with all its complications and obscurities. And at this belated hour, when in South Africa every moment pulsed and throbbed with fate, they asked for further information concerning the original proposals for joint enquiry into franchise details and for subsequent conference on other matters. That olive branch was tendered at the end of July. Now was the beginning of September. There was a gulf between. And still the Boer Government did not accept joint enquiry. They only awaited further information. Another vista was opened of interminable delay and hopeless uncertainty. It was more than British repute in South Africa could now bear or British opinion at home endure.

Reform in the Transvaal or War

ALFRED MILNER

[The following letter, written in February, 1898, more than a year and a half before the outbreak of war, indicates Milner's assessment of the situation at that time.]

LETTER FROM SIR A. MILNER TO
MR. CHAMBERLAIN

23/2/98. The long despatch which goes to you by this mail about our differences with the Transvaal, is written with a purpose. I am afraid that after a few months' respite, we are once more on the verge of serious trouble with the Boers; the despatch is one which, if things get worse, it may be useful some day to publish. But of course, *only if things get worse.* My reason in writing this letter is to warn you privately, that I think there is a very great probability that they will. There is no way out of the political troubles of S. Africa except reform in the Transvaal or war. And at present the chances of reform in the Transvaal are worse than ever. The Boers quarrel bitterly amongst themselves, but it is about jobs and contracts, not politics! In their determination to keep all power in their own hands and to use it with a total disregard of the interests of the unenfranchised, as well as in their own hatred and suspicion of Great Britain, the vast majority of them are firmly united. There is absolutely no sign of amendment in these respects. For a few months after I came here things began to look a little better. I began to hope that we might get, not indeed on to good, but on to tolerable terms with them, that though the fundamental antagonism might remain unaltered, a few minor concessions on their part, a few small courtesies on ours, might serve to conceal it, to allow us to attend to our own business, and them to muddle on in their own way, and ultimately to develop political parties amongst themselves, which would compete for the support of the Uitlander. These hopes have so far been disappointed, and since the beginning of the autumn — when Leyds returned — any little signs of consideration for the subject races of the Transvaal, whether European or native, and of civility to us, have ceased to appear. Schalk Burger has proved a broken reed. Kruger has returned to power, more autocratic and more reactionary than ever. It would not be surprising if he suffered from megalomania, seeing what he started from and where he now is. He has immense resources in money and any amount of ammunitions of war, to which he is constantly adding. Politically, he has strengthened his hold on the Orange Free State, and the Colonial Afrikanders continue to do obeisance before him. And not only the Afrikanders. He has been congratulated on his re-election by an unanimous vote of the Bond. But what is more eye-opening, he has also received a congratulatory telegram from Binns, the British Prime Minister of Natal. Under these circumstances, I conceive that it depends entirely on Leyds' estimate of the general European situation, whether we do or do not get an embarrassingly rude answer to the despatch on the Suzerainty question. Of one thing I am quite certain. Kruger will never take any step which he thinks will provoke us to fight. But if he is assured that our hands are full in other directions he will certainly seize the opportunity to assert his independence in a very pointed way. . . . *Looking*

From *The Milner Papers*, Vol. I, *South Africa, 1897–1899*, ed. Cecil Headlam (London, 1931), pp. 220–223; 267–268; 348–349; 351–353; 384–385; 445. Reprinted by permission of Cassell & Co., Ltd., A. P. Watt & Son, and of New College, Oxford.

at the question from a purely S. African point of view, I should be inclined to work up to a crisis, not indeed by looking about for causes of complaint or making a fuss about trifles, but by steadily and inflexibly pressing for the redress of substantial wrongs and injustices. It would not be difficult thus to work up an extremely strong *cumulative case*. The questions already under discussion almost constitute one. Throw in the dynamite monopoly — about which I have not yet moved, the treatment of Cape Boys which is something like a breach of promise, and the numberless cases of petty tyranny to Natives or Europeans in Swaziland or elsewhere which are always cropping up, but which as a rule we do not bother about, and the case is more than adequate. But the drawback to this policy is that it puts the choice of the time, when we may be forced to take strong aggressive action, out of our hands. As long as we merely remonstrate about this, that, or the other in a perfunctory sort of way, we can, if we get unsatisfactory answers, or no answers, afford to assume a manner of indifference. But if we are going to remonstrate incisively, to insist on being answered promptly and unevasively — in short to show that we mean business — then we cannot disregard either a persistent silence or a flat refusal. It means that we shall have to fight, and to fight *more or less* at a moment chosen by the other side, who very likely may not realize what they are doing. The question, which line to take cannot therefore be settled exclusively with reference to S. Africa. *It depends on the Imperial outlook as a whole.*

*   *   *

EXTRACT FROM LETTER. SIR A. MILNER
TO MR. CHAMBERLAIN

6/7/98. [CONFIDENTIAL] Your telegram about Delagoa Bay. . . . I look on possession of Delagoa Bay as the best chance we have of winning the great game between ourselves and the Transvaal for the mastery in South Africa without a war. I am not indeed sure that we shall ever be masters

without a war. The more I see of S.A. the more I doubt it. But if we are not to fight and yet not to be worsted, one of 2 things must happen. Either Rhodesia must develop *very* rapidly, or we must get Delagoa Bay. Now the *very rapid* development of Rhodesia is more than doubtful. I believe it is going to develop and be a possession worth having, but I do not believe it is going to be a rival to the Transvaal for many years to come. And in that case I fear that the overwhelming preponderance in wealth and opportunity on the side of the Transvaal may turn the scale against us, unless we have some means to bring very effective pressure to bear upon that country. There is none that I can see except the command of all its trade routes of which I need not tell you that Delagoa Bay is the most important.

*   *   *

[*The following letter to Lord Selborne, Under-Secretary of State for the Colonies, preceded Milner's famous "helots" telegram of May 4th, portions of which are quoted below.*]

EXTRACT FROM LETTER. SIR A. MILNER
TO LORD SELBORNE

5/4/99. . . . My own view is in my secret despatches — only not quite so strongly put as what I really feel. I don't want to give you the impression that *I wish to rush you.* And I am painfully conscious that what is to us all here an all-overshadowing nightmare, precluding any other work of a more useful kind, is to people at home a matter of faint interest exciting only a very small degree of public attention. It is odd that it should be so, seeing the enormous material value of the thing involved, as well as the plainness of the moral issues. But so it apparently is. What I wish particularly is that all this mass of material, which we are pouring into you, may not go wholly unutilized for the instruction of the public, even if it produces no impression at all — on the action of the Govt. Then one's time will not have been wholly wasted in the long run. Will you not publish a Blue Book and see that Edgar shootings and Jones trials, amphitheatre meetings, Lombaard incidents, etc., etc., etc., get rubbed into the public mind. I wish to goodness some of my vitriol could get in too. But I am afraid to put too much vitriol into public despatches, lest they should never see the light of day. And my secret despatches, which have all the stuff in them, are, I suppose, from the nature of the case unproducible, even in part. P.S. — Don't be afraid of publishing anything lest it should annoy the Transvaal and Afrikanders. They are already *furious* with you. But, on the other hand, if we never mean, not only *now* but at any future time, to do anything, it is useless to call general attention to our impotence by barking. Of course, I always assume that the time will and must come. Otherwise life would be unbearable.

Such was the origin of the famous telegram of May 4, a document which has been described by Sir Charles Lucas as "broad and far-seeing in a rare degree," and by Mr. Amery, as "one of the most masterly State documents ever penned." In terse, frank phrases the High Commissioner set before H. M. Government and the wide public of the British Empire the whole case of the Second Reform Movement, and the reasons for his conclusion that "the case for intervention is overwhelming." And in one passage, inspired by the clear vision of a great and courageous Statesman, he insisted upon the essential unity of South Africa, and the folly of one of the two white races, "everywhere inextricably mixed up" therein, dreaming of subjugating the other.

TELEGRAM FROM SIR A. MILNER
TO MR. CHAMBERLAIN

4th May. Having regard to critical character of South African situation and likelihood of early reply by Her Majesty's Government to Petition, I am telegraphing remarks which under ordinary circumstances I should have made by despatch. Events of importance have followed so fast on each other since my return to South Africa, and my time has been so fully occupied in dealing with each incident severally, that I have had no opportunity for reviewing the whole position. . . .

A busy industrial community is not naturally prone to political unrest. But they bear the chief burden of taxation; they constantly feel in their business and daily lives the effects of chaotic legislation and of incompetent and unsympathetic administration; they have many grievances, but they believe all this could be gradually removed if they had only a fair share of political power. This is the meaning of their vehement demand for enfranchisement. Moreover, they are mostly British subjects, accustomed to a free system and equal rights; they feel deeply the personal indignity involved in position of permanent subjection to the ruling caste which owes its wealth and power to their exertion. The political turmoil in the Transvaal Republic will never end till the permanent Uitlander population is admitted to a share in the Government, and while that turmoil lasts there will be no tranquillity or adequate progress in Her Majesty's South African dominions.

The relations between the British Colonies and the two Republics are intimate to a degree which one must live in South Africa in order fully to realize. Socially, economically, ethnologically, they are all one country, the two principal white races are everywhere inextricably mixed up; it is absurd for either to dream of subjugating the other. The only condition on which they can live in harmony and the country progress is equality all round. South Africa can prosper under two, three, or six Governments, though the fewer the better, but not under two absolutely conflicting social and political systems, perfect equality for Dutch and British in the British Colonies side by side with permanent subjection of British to Dutch in one of the Republics. It is idle to talk of peace and unity under such a state of affairs. . . .

The true remedy is to strike at the root

of all these injuries, the political impotence of the injured. What diplomatic protests will never accomplish, a fair measure of Uitlander representation would gradually but surely bring about. It seems a paradox but it is true that the only effective way of protecting our subjects is to help them to cease to be our subjects. The admission of Uitlanders to a fair share of political power would no doubt give stability to the Republic. But it would at the same time remove most of our causes of difference with it, and modify and in the long run entirely remove that intense suspicion and bitter hostility to Great Britain which at present dominates its internal and external policy.

The case for intervention is overwhelming. The only attempted answer is that things will right themselves if left alone. But, in fact, the policy of leaving things alone has been tried for years, and it has led to their going from bad to worse. It is not true that this is owing to the Raid. They were going from bad to worse before the Raid. We were on the verge of war before the Raid, and the Transvaal was on the verge of revolution. The effect of the Raid has been to give the policy of leaving things alone a new lease of life, and with the old consequences. . . .

The spectacle of thousands of British subjects kept permanently in the position of helots, constantly chafing under undoubted grievances, and calling vainly to Her Majesty's Government for redress, does steadily undermine the influence and reputation of Great Britain and the respect for the British Government within its own dominions. A certain section of the press, and not in the Transvaal only, preaches openly and constantly the doctrine of a Republic embracing all South Africa, and supports it by menacing references to the armaments of the Transvaal, its alliance with the Orange Free State, and the active sympathy which in case of war it would receive from a section of Her Majesty's subjects. I regret to say that this doctrine, supported as it is by a ceaseless stream of malignant lies about the intentions of the British Government, is producing a great effect upon a large number of our Dutch fellow-colonists. Language is frequently used which seems to imply that the Dutch have some superior right even in this colony to their fellow-citizens of British birth. Thousands of men peaceably disposed, and, if left alone, perfectly satisfied with their position as British subjects, are being drawn into disaffection, and there is a corresponding exasperation on the side of the British.

I can see nothing which will put a stop to this mischievous propaganda but some striking proof of the intention, if it is the intention, of Her Majesty's Government not to be ousted from its position in South Africa. And the best proof alike of its power and its justice would be to obtain for the Uitlanders in the Transvaal a fair share in the Government of the country which owes everything to their exertions. It could be made perfectly clear that our action was not directed against the existence of the Republic. We should only be demanding the re-establishment of rights which now exist in the Orange Free State, and which existed in the Transvaal itself at the time of and long after the withdrawal of British sovereignty. It would be no selfish demand, as other Uitlanders besides those of British birth would benefit by it. It is asking for nothing from others which we do not give ourselves. And it would certainly go to the root of the political unrest in South Africa, and, though temporarily it might aggravate, it would ultimately extinguish the race feud which is the great bane of the country.

*   *   *

[The following letter was written by Milner shortly before his meeting with Kruger at the Bloemfontein Conference, May 31– June 5, 1899.]

EXTRACT FROM LETTER. SIR A. MILNER
TO LORD SELBORNE

17/5/99. Excitement here much greater than anything I have known since coming to S. Africa. It is difficult to imagine how things will look when this letter reaches you in 2–3 weeks' time. . . . Now I don't want war, but I admit I begin to think it may be the only way out. . . . No use saying now what I shall try to get out of old Kruger. Our interview will probably be over before this reaches you. But, as at present advised, I think I ought to be *very stiff* about Uitlander grievances and put my demands on this subject high — though they may seem high to Kruger, they would be called very moderate in England — and get him to break off, if he does break off, on these, rather than on any one of the 101 other differences, which, though they may afford better technical *casus belli,* do not really *mean so much* or excite so much interest. *Nota bene.* The meetings in Australia in support of Uitlanders' complaints are important facts. This objection of ours to the *permanent inferiority* of men of British race is a strong point. The great question will come when I have seen Kruger — and failed to get anything substantial out of him. Mind you, I mean to try all I know, but as no one has ever yet succeeded with him in all these many years, it really is a little too much to hope that I shall. If I fail, it will then be *your* turn. Now, I don't wish to exaggerate, and I know all your difficulties, but I am fully convinced that, if we make *no substantial progress* after all this fearful row and effort — and now that the public mind here is so excited — it will take us years to recover such a fiasco if we ever recover it. The thing will be the more exasperating because we really are so near a big success. The Boers and their sympathizers have never been in such a funk for many years — never since Warren's expedition.

Therefore my advice to you is, if I fail with Kruger, to assume at once the diplomatic offensive and to back it with a strong show of material force. We shall need all our moral pluck then out here, for we are surrounded by enemies. All the Afrikanders and all the mugwumps will howl at us in the Faure style — the former practically threatening us with rebellion, the latter

with the terrible consequences of victory. I don't care. My view is, (1) that absolute downright determination plus a large temporary increase of force will ensure a climb down. It is 20 to 1. And (2) that, if it didn't and there was a fight, it would be better to fight now than 5 or 10 years hence, when the Transvaal, unless the Uitlanders can be taken in, in considerable numbers, will be stronger and more hostile than ever.

* * *

[*The following letter from Lord Selborne to Milner concerns the state of public opinion in Britain in June, 1899.*]

EXTRACT FROM LETTER. LORD SELBORNE
TO SIR A. MILNER

25/6/99. [CONFIDENTIAL] This is a plain business letter to fill up gaps in your knowledge of what has happened here. The warnings Mr. C. and I gave you about the state of public opinion here have been abundantly justified. The publication of the Blue Book produced a great effect but not so great an effect as we had hoped. The idea of war with the S.A.R. is very distasteful to most people. Consequently the Cabinet have undoubtedly had to modify the pace that they contemplated moving at immediately after the Bloemfontein Conference. There is no idea of receding from the intervention which was commenced by your action at Bloemfontein and our reply to the petition, but we simply cannot force the pace. We have between us moved public opinion, almost universally, forward to the position of accepting the eventual responsibility of seeing a remedy applied, and this is a great step forward; but we have not convinced them yet either that you can't believe a word Kruger says, or that he never has yielded and never will yield till he feels the muzzle of the pistol on his forehead, or that the surest way to avoid war is to prepare openly for war. Now you see where we are — Mr. C. speaks to his constituents at Birmingham to-morrow and I have implored him to give public opinion a lead and I think he will, but I need not tell you that the worst service we could do the Empire would be to outrun public opinion. We may have to go more slowly than you or we know would be wisest, and all protraction of the crisis adds to its difficulty, but so long as we never turn back you must trust us sufficiently to pardon an occasional dawdle. We have entered a lane, you have entered a lane, the Cabinet has entered a lane, the country has entered a lane, where no turning back is possible without humiliation and disaster.

While the readings in this book may serve as an introduction to issues and interpretations concerning the Anglo-Boer War, they constitute only a beginning. For any comprehensive and thorough study of major points, an extensive body of historical writings and sources must be consulted. The list which follows is quite selective and will point the way to the more significant materials.

A wealth of information on the history of South Africa as a whole is contained in the second edition of *The Cambridge History of the British Empire,* Vol. VIII: *South Africa* (Cambridge, 1963), edited by the eminent historian of South Africa, Eric A. Walker. His chapter on "The Struggle for Supremacy, 1896–1902," and his section on "The Jameson Raid" incorporate the results of recent research. This book also contains an admirable bibliography, the most recent and comprehensive on South African history, including manuscript collections and official papers and publications, as well as secondary writings. The section on historical materials in Britain was done by A. Taylor Milne and that on materials in Southern Africa by A. C. G. Lloyd. Another informative general work is E. A. Walker's *History of Southern Africa* (3rd ed., London, 1957), while his published lecture, "Lord Milner and South Africa," *Proceedings of the British Academy,* XXVIII (1942), is interesting and stimulating; he has also edited a *Historical Atlas of South Africa* (Cape Town, 1922), which is useful. Two books by C. W. de Kiewiet are excellent on the aspects which they treat: *A History of South Africa, Social and Economic* (Oxford, 1941), and *The Imperial Factor in South Africa* (Cambridge, 1937), which deals with the 1870's and '80's. A recent narrative account of the war itself is by Rayne Kruger, *Good-bye Dolly Gray: The Story of the Boer War* (London, 1959), vividly written and based

on considerable knowledge. Also useful is Edgar Holt, *The Boer War* (London, 1958), which deals mainly with military aspects. Much more comprehensive is *"The Times" History of the War in South Africa, 1899–1902* (7 vols., London, 1900–1909), edited by L. S. Amery.

If the war is to be viewed in its proper setting, it is necessary to understand the attitude of the British people toward their empire, and the evolution of imperial ideas in general. A good, brief introduction is contained in Chapter X of *The Cambridge History of the British Empire,* Vol. III: *The Empire Commonwealth, 1870–1919,* eds. E. A. Benians, Sir James Butler, and C. E. Carrington (Cambridge, 1959). More detailed and quite cogent in treatment are two recent works: Ronald Robinson and John Gallagher, with Alice Denny, *Africa and the Victorians: The Official Mind of Imperialism* (London, 1961), and A. P. Thornton, *The Imperial Idea and Its Enemies* (London, 1959). Both concentrate on the "official" mind rather than on public opinion. Good on the story of imperialism and on concepts of empire is Richard Koebner and H. D. Schmidt, *Imperialism: The Story and Significance of a Political Word, 1840–1960* (Cambridge, 1964). Two useful books of readings on the topic of imperialism, both of which contain bibliographies, are Robin W. Winks, *British Imperialism: Gold, God, Glory* (New York, 1963), and Harrison M. Wright, *The "New Imperialism": Analysis of Late Nineteenth-Century Expansion* (Boston, 1961). William L. Strauss, *Joseph Chamberlain and the Theory of Imperialism* (Washington, 1942) treats the imperial ideas of that important figure. Of many articles, three are listed here: Eric Stokes, "Great Britain and Africa: The Myth of Imperialism," *History Today,* X (1960), 554–63; also by Stokes, "Milnerism," *The Historical Journal,* V (1962), 47–60; and N. G. Garson,

"British Imperialism and the Coming of the Anglo-Boer War," *South African Journal of Economics*, XXX (1962), 140–53.

By far the most thorough detailed study of developments between 1895 and 1899 is that of J. S. Marais, *The Fall of Kruger's Republic* (Oxford, 1961). New material was contained in the article by Ethel Drus, "Select Documents from the Chamberlain Papers concerning Anglo-Transvaal Relations, 1896–1899," *Bulletin of the Institute of Historical Research*, XXVII (1954), 156–89. The book by Reginald I. Lovell, *The Struggle for South Africa, 1875–1899* (New York, 1934) is of value in relating South African events to the context of European diplomacy in that period, as also is the article by C. D. Penner, "Germany and the Transvaal before 1896," *Journal of Modern History*, XII (1940), 31–58. A study which grew out of a doctoral dissertation is that of R. H. Wilde, *Joseph Chamberlain and the South African Republic, 1895–1899*, in *Archives Year Book for South Africa, 1956* (Pretoria, 1956).

The detailed and scholarly study by Jean van der Poel, *The Jameson Raid* (London, 1951) must be given first rank on that topic. The book by Elizabeth Pakenham, *Jameson's Raid* (London, 1960) is an entertaining account which disagrees on some points with the conclusions of Miss van der Poel. New evidence was added by Ethel Drus in her article, "A Report on the Private Papers of Joseph Chamberlain Relating to the Jameson Raid and the Inquiry," *Bulletin of the Institute of Historical Research*, XXV (1952), 33–62. Additional material from the papers of Cecil Rhodes and a summary of recent evidence on this detective story is contained in articles by C. M. Woodhouse, "The Missing Telegrams and The Jameson Raid," *History Today*, XII (June, 1962), 395–404, and (July, 1962), 506–14.

Biographies of leading figures on both the Boer and British sides are of great interest in themselves and they throw a highly valuable light on the attitudes and ideas of men and groups, as well as on events themselves. Of the many lives of Cecil Rhodes, two recent ones are perhaps the most useful: J. G. Lockhart and C. M. Woodhouse, *Rhodes* (London, 1963), and Felix Gross, *Rhodes of Africa* (London, 1956). A useful bibliography on Rhodes is that of E. E. Burke, comp., *A Bibliography of Cecil John Rhodes* (Salisbury, Southern Rhodesia, 1952). J. L. Garvin's *Life of Joseph Chamberlain* (3 vols., London, 1931–4), with volume IV by Julian Amery (London, 1951), although uncritical in parts, has exceptional value. There is as yet no comprehensive life of Milner, but three works, all favorable to him, are quite useful on certain aspects of his career: V. Halpérin, *Lord Milner and the Empire* [trans.] (London, 1952), E. Crankshaw, *The Forsaken Idea, a Study of Viscount Milner* (London, 1952), and Sir John Evelyn Wrench, *Alfred Lord Milner: The Man of No Illusions* (London, 1958). The work of I. Colvin, *The Life of Jameson* (2 vols., London, 1923), deals with that rather colorful personality. Two biographies by Eric A. Walker are particularly valuable on the ideas and role of the Cape Dutch: *W. P. Schreiner, a South African* (London, 1937), and *Lord de Villiers and His Times* (London, 1925), as also is J. H. Hofmeyr's, *The Life of Jan Hendrik Hofmeyr* (Cape Town, 1913). E. T. Cook's *Edmund Garrett, a Memoir* (London, 1909), contains revealing information on the editor of the *Cape Times*. The following biographies of leaders on the Boer side are interesting and useful, although they deal for the most part with events subsequent to the war: F. V. Englenburg, *General Louis Botha* (London, 1929), Sir W. K. Hancock, *Smuts: The Sanguine Years, 1870–1919* (Cambridge, 1962), based largely on documents in the Smuts Archive; J. C. Smuts, *Jan Christian Smuts* (London, 1952), and N. J. van der Merwe, *Marthinus Theunis Steyn* (2 vols., Cape Town, 1921).

A considerable number of contemporary observers saw fit to write descriptive and critical accounts which add appreciably to the understanding of conditions in South

Africa. In addition to those which are quoted in this book, one of the most acute was that of James Bryce, *Impressions of South Africa* (3rd ed., New York, 1900), which contains comments written from a liberal viewpoint and is cautiously critical of the British position. More influential at the time was the widely read book by the South African leader, Percy Fitzpatrick, *The Transvaal from Within* (London, 1899). Written from a viewpoint quite hostile to Kruger and his policies, this book was credited with helping to convince many Britons in 1899, including Lord Salisbury, of the justice of their cause. The correspondent of *The Times* in South Africa, Sir Francis Younghusband wrote *South Africa Today* (London, 1898), a book which contains revealing sidelights. The following memoirs throw light on various aspects: Sir William Butler, *Autobiography* (London, 1911), unsympathetic with British policy; Sir James Rose-Innes, *Autobiography* (Cape Town, 1949); J. G. Kotzé, *Biographical Memoirs and Reminiscences* (2 vols., Cape Town, 1934–41); Percy Fitzpatrick, *South African Memories* (London, 1932); and K. van Hoek [transcriber], *Kruger Days: Reminiscences of Dr. Leyds* (London, 1939). *The Memoirs of Paul Kruger* (2 vols., New York, 1902) express his point of view, but add little in the way of information.

A good introduction to pamphlet literature of the time is the article by John S. Galbraith, "The Pamphlet Campaign of the Boer War," *Journal of Modern History*, XXIV (June, 1952), 111–26. Joseph O. Baylen's "W. T. Stead and the Boer War, the Irony of Idealism," *Canadian Historical Review*, XL (1959), 304–14, deals with one of the leading pamphleteers. At the time of the war articles of opinion appeared in most leading periodicals, such as *Contemporary Review, Nineteenth Century, Fortnightly Review, Edinburgh Review*, and the *Review of Reviews*. Of this extensive literature, the following examples are useful for the light they throw on conditions or on contemporary opinion: James Bryce, "The Historical Causes of the Present War in South Africa," *North American Review*, CLXIX (December, 1899), 737–59; F. Edmund Garrett, "The Inevitable in South Africa," *Contemporary Review* (October, 1899), 457–81; Sidney Shippard, "Are We to Lose South Africa?" *Nineteenth Century*, XLVI (July, 1899), 1–7.

In the end, a realistic understanding of how the war came can best be obtained through careful examination of the primary source materials. Sources of all types for South Africa, including manuscript collections now available, are listed systematically in the bibliography, to which reference is made above, in *The Cambridge History of the British Empire*, Vol. VIII. Of particular value for events of 1899 are the Parliamentary Papers, for they contain official correspondence and reports which provide a remarkably revealing picture of the developing crisis. The following papers for 1899 should be consulted: LXIV: [C.9345] dealing with complaints of British subjects in the South African Republic, 1897–99; LXIV: [C.9404], [C.9415], [C.9518], [C.9521], [C.9530], on the Bloemfontein Conference and proposed political reforms; and LXIV: [C.9507] which deals with the status of the South African Republic, 1899.